50 New Years Dinner Recipes for Home

By: Kelly Johnson

Table of Contents

- Roasted Beef Tenderloin
- Honey Glazed Ham
- Garlic Herb Crusted Rack of Lamb
- Baked Salmon with Dill Sauce
- Shrimp Scampi
- Stuffed Portobello Mushrooms
- Lobster Mac and Cheese
- Chicken Marsala
- Beef Wellington
- Butternut Squash Risotto
- Mediterranean Stuffed Bell Peppers
- Lobster Tail with Lemon Butter
- Cranberry Orange Glazed Pork
- Teriyaki Glazed Salmon
- Spinach and Artichoke Stuffed Chicken
- Garlic Butter Shrimp
- Beef Stroganoff
- Creamy Mushroom Soup
- Maple Glazed Carrots
- Roasted Brussels Sprouts with Bacon
- Parmesan Crusted Chicken
- Creamy Spinach and Ricotta Stuffed Shells
- Balsamic Glazed Steak
- Herb Roasted Turkey Breast
- Lemon Herb Chicken Thighs
- Truffle Mac and Cheese
- Pomegranate Glazed Pork Chops
- Roasted Cauliflower with Parmesan
- Buttery Garlic Mashed Potatoes
- Prosciutto Wrapped Asparagus
- Sweet Potato and Black Bean Enchiladas
- Crab Cakes with Remoulade Sauce
- Chicken Alfredo Pasta
- Mediterranean Quinoa Salad
- Beef Bourguignon
- Honey Mustard Glazed Carrots

- Lobster Newberg
- Baked Ziti with Sausage
- Parmesan Crusted Salmon
- Stuffed Acorn Squash
- Sautéed Green Beans with Almonds
- Bacon-Wrapped Dates
- Grilled Vegetable Platter
- Classic Beef Chili
- Shrimp and Grits
- Thai Green Curry with Chicken
- Spaghetti Carbonara
- Pumpkin Sage Risotto
- Baked Chicken Parmesan
- Roasted Garlic Mashed Potatoes

Roasted Beef Tenderloin

Ingredients

- **1 (3-4 pound) beef tenderloin**, trimmed
- **2 tablespoons olive oil**
- **3 tablespoons Dijon mustard**
- **4 cloves garlic**, minced
- **1 tablespoon fresh rosemary**, chopped
- **1 tablespoon fresh thyme**, chopped
- **1 tablespoon salt**
- **1 teaspoon black pepper**
- **1 teaspoon paprika**
- **1 teaspoon onion powder**
- **1 teaspoon garlic powder**

Instructions

1. **Preheat Oven:**
   - Preheat your oven to 425°F (220°C).
2. **Prepare the Beef:**
   - Pat the beef tenderloin dry with paper towels. This helps to get a good sear and seasoning adherence.
3. **Seasoning Mixture:**
   - In a small bowl, mix together the Dijon mustard, minced garlic, rosemary, thyme, salt, pepper, paprika, onion powder, and garlic powder.
4. **Apply Seasoning:**
   - Rub the seasoning mixture evenly all over the beef tenderloin.
5. **Sear the Beef:**
   - Heat the olive oil in a large, oven-proof skillet over medium-high heat. Once hot, add the beef tenderloin and sear on all sides until browned, about 2-3 minutes per side.
6. **Roast:**
   - Transfer the skillet to the preheated oven. Roast the beef tenderloin for 20-25 minutes, or until an internal thermometer reads 130°F (54°C) for medium-rare or 140°F (60°C) for medium.
7. **Rest:**
   - Remove the beef from the oven and transfer it to a cutting board. Let it rest for 10-15 minutes before slicing. This allows the juices to redistribute throughout the meat.
8. **Serve:**
   - Slice the beef tenderloin into medallions and serve with your favorite sides.

Enjoy your perfectly roasted beef tenderloin!

Honey Glazed Ham

Ingredients

- 1 (8-10 pound) fully cooked bone-in ham
- 1 cup honey
- 1/2 cup brown sugar
- 1/4 cup Dijon mustard
- 1/4 cup apple cider vinegar
- 1/4 cup orange juice
- 1/2 teaspoon ground cloves
- 1/2 teaspoon ground cinnamon
- 1/4 teaspoon ground nutmeg

Instructions

1. **Preheat Oven:**
   - Preheat your oven to 325°F (163°C).
2. **Prepare the Ham:**
   - Remove the ham from its packaging and discard the skin. Place the ham, cut side down, in a roasting pan. If the ham has a rind, score it with a knife in a diamond pattern.
3. **Prepare Glaze:**
   - In a medium saucepan, combine the honey, brown sugar, Dijon mustard, apple cider vinegar, orange juice, ground cloves, cinnamon, and nutmeg. Bring the mixture to a boil over medium heat, stirring frequently. Reduce the heat and simmer for 5-7 minutes, or until the glaze has thickened slightly.
4. **Glaze the Ham:**
   - Brush the ham generously with the honey glaze, making sure to get some glaze between the scored sections if applicable.
5. **Roast the Ham:**
   - Cover the roasting pan loosely with aluminum foil and place it in the preheated oven. Roast for 1.5 to 2 hours, basting the ham with additional glaze every 30 minutes.
6. **Finish Glazing:**
   - During the last 30 minutes of roasting, remove the foil and increase the oven temperature to 400°F (204°C). Brush the ham with more glaze and roast uncovered until the glaze is caramelized and the ham is heated through. An internal temperature of 140°F (60°C) is ideal.
7. **Rest:**
   - Remove the ham from the oven and let it rest for 10-15 minutes before carving. This allows the juices to redistribute and makes slicing easier.
8. **Serve:**
   - Carve the ham into slices and serve with the remaining honey glaze on the side.

Enjoy your sweet and savory honey-glazed ham!

Garlic Herb Crusted Rack of Lamb

Ingredients

- **1 (8-rib) rack of lamb**, frenched
- **3 tablespoons olive oil**
- **4 cloves garlic**, minced
- **2 tablespoons fresh rosemary**, chopped
- **2 tablespoons fresh thyme**, chopped
- **1 tablespoon Dijon mustard**
- **1 tablespoon fresh parsley**, chopped (optional for garnish)
- **1 teaspoon salt**
- **1/2 teaspoon black pepper**
- **1/2 cup breadcrumbs** (preferably panko for extra crunch)
- **2 tablespoons grated Parmesan cheese**

Instructions

1. **Preheat Oven:**
   - Preheat your oven to 400°F (200°C).
2. **Prepare the Rack of Lamb:**
   - Pat the rack of lamb dry with paper towels. This helps the seasoning stick and ensures a good sear.
3. **Season the Rack:**
   - In a small bowl, mix together the minced garlic, rosemary, thyme, Dijon mustard, salt, and black pepper. Rub this mixture all over the lamb, making sure to cover it evenly.
4. **Sear the Lamb:**
   - Heat olive oil in a large, oven-proof skillet over medium-high heat. Once hot, add the rack of lamb and sear for 2-3 minutes on each side until browned. This helps to lock in the flavors.
5. **Prepare the Herb Crust:**
   - In a separate bowl, combine the breadcrumbs and Parmesan cheese. Press this mixture onto the top of the lamb to form an even crust.
6. **Roast:**
   - Transfer the skillet with the lamb to the preheated oven. Roast for 15-20 minutes, or until the internal temperature reaches 125°F (52°C) for rare, 135°F (57°C) for medium-rare, or 145°F (63°C) for medium. The exact time will vary based on the size of the rack and your desired doneness.
7. **Rest:**
   - Remove the rack from the oven and let it rest for 10 minutes before carving. This allows the juices to redistribute, making the meat tender and juicy.
8. **Serve:**
   - Slice the rack into individual chops and garnish with fresh parsley if desired. Serve with your favorite side dishes.

Enjoy your beautifully roasted garlic herb crusted rack of lamb!

Baked Salmon with Dill Sauce

Ingredients

- **4 (6-ounce) salmon fillets**
- **2 tablespoons olive oil**
- **1 tablespoon lemon juice**
- **1 teaspoon garlic powder**
- **1 teaspoon onion powder**
- **1 teaspoon dried dill**
- **Salt and black pepper to taste**

For the Dill Sauce:

- **1/2 cup sour cream**
- **1/4 cup mayonnaise**
- **1 tablespoon fresh dill**, chopped (or 1 teaspoon dried dill)
- **1 tablespoon lemon juice**
- **1 teaspoon Dijon mustard**
- **1 small garlic clove**, minced
- **Salt and black pepper to taste**

Instructions

1. **Preheat Oven:**
   - Preheat your oven to 400°F (200°C).
2. **Prepare the Salmon:**
   - Line a baking sheet with parchment paper or lightly grease it with olive oil. Place the salmon fillets on the prepared baking sheet.
   - Drizzle olive oil and lemon juice over the salmon. Season with garlic powder, onion powder, dried dill, salt, and black pepper.
3. **Bake the Salmon:**
   - Bake the salmon in the preheated oven for 12-15 minutes, or until the salmon flakes easily with a fork. The cooking time will depend on the thickness of the fillets.
4. **Prepare the Dill Sauce:**
   - While the salmon is baking, mix together the sour cream, mayonnaise, fresh dill, lemon juice, Dijon mustard, minced garlic, salt, and black pepper in a bowl. Adjust seasoning to taste.
5. **Serve:**
   - Remove the salmon from the oven and let it rest for a few minutes. Serve the salmon fillets with a generous dollop of dill sauce on top or on the side.

Enjoy your delicious baked salmon with a creamy dill sauce!

Shrimp Scampi

Ingredients

- **1 pound large shrimp**, peeled and deveined
- **8 ounces linguine** or spaghetti
- **4 tablespoons unsalted butter**
- **2 tablespoons olive oil**
- **4 cloves garlic**, minced
- **1/4 teaspoon red pepper flakes** (adjust to taste)
- **1/2 cup white wine** or chicken broth
- **Juice of 1 lemon**
- **Zest of 1 lemon**
- **1/4 cup fresh parsley**, chopped
- **Salt and black pepper to taste**
- **Grated Parmesan cheese** (optional, for serving)

Instructions

1. **Cook the Pasta:**
   - Cook the linguine or spaghetti according to package instructions until al dente. Drain and set aside, reserving 1/2 cup of pasta water.
2. **Prepare the Shrimp:**
   - Pat the shrimp dry with paper towels. Season with a pinch of salt and black pepper.
3. **Cook the Shrimp:**
   - In a large skillet, heat the olive oil and 2 tablespoons of butter over medium-high heat. Add the shrimp in a single layer and cook for about 2-3 minutes on each side, or until they turn pink and opaque. Remove the shrimp from the skillet and set aside.
4. **Make the Scampi Sauce:**
   - In the same skillet, add the remaining 2 tablespoons of butter. Once melted, add the minced garlic and red pepper flakes. Sauté for about 1 minute, until fragrant.
   - Pour in the white wine or chicken broth and lemon juice. Scrape up any browned bits from the bottom of the skillet with a wooden spoon. Let the sauce simmer for 2-3 minutes, allowing it to reduce slightly.
5. **Combine:**
   - Return the shrimp to the skillet and toss to coat in the sauce. Add the lemon zest and chopped parsley. Cook for an additional minute to heat the shrimp through.
6. **Add Pasta:**
   - Add the cooked pasta to the skillet and toss everything together. If the sauce is too thick, add a little of the reserved pasta water to reach the desired consistency.
7. **Serve:**
   - Serve the shrimp scampi immediately, garnished with extra parsley and grated Parmesan cheese if desired.

Enjoy your flavorful and buttery shrimp scampi!

Stuffed Portobello Mushrooms

Ingredients

- **4 large Portobello mushrooms**
- **2 tablespoons olive oil**
- **1 small onion**, finely chopped
- **2 cloves garlic**, minced
- **1/2 cup bell pepper**, finely chopped (any color)
- **1/2 cup cherry tomatoes**, halved
- **1/2 cup spinach**, chopped
- **1/4 cup sun-dried tomatoes**, chopped
- **1/2 cup breadcrumbs** (preferably panko for extra crunch)
- **1/4 cup grated Parmesan cheese**
- **1/4 cup shredded mozzarella cheese**
- **1 tablespoon fresh basil**, chopped (or 1 teaspoon dried basil)
- **1 tablespoon fresh parsley**, chopped (or 1 teaspoon dried parsley)
- **Salt and black pepper to taste**
- **1 teaspoon balsamic vinegar** (optional)

Instructions

1. **Preheat Oven:**
   - Preheat your oven to 375°F (190°C).
2. **Prepare the Mushrooms:**
   - Gently clean the Portobello mushrooms with a damp paper towel. Remove the stems and scoop out the gills using a spoon to create a cavity for the stuffing. Lightly brush the mushroom caps with olive oil and place them, stem side up, on a baking sheet.
3. **Prepare the Filling:**
   - In a skillet, heat 1 tablespoon of olive oil over medium heat. Add the chopped onion and garlic, and sauté for about 2 minutes until they become translucent.
   - Add the bell pepper and cook for an additional 3-4 minutes until softened.
   - Stir in the cherry tomatoes, spinach, and sun-dried tomatoes. Cook for another 2 minutes, just until the spinach is wilted. Remove from heat and let cool slightly.
4. **Mix the Stuffing:**
   - In a bowl, combine the sautéed vegetables with breadcrumbs, Parmesan cheese, mozzarella cheese, basil, parsley, salt, and black pepper. Mix well until everything is evenly distributed.
5. **Stuff the Mushrooms:**
   - Spoon the filling evenly into each Portobello mushroom cap, pressing it down gently to pack it in.
6. **Bake:**

- Drizzle the remaining tablespoon of olive oil over the stuffed mushrooms. Bake in the preheated oven for 20-25 minutes, or until the mushrooms are tender and the tops are golden brown.
7. **Finish and Serve:**
   - If desired, drizzle a small amount of balsamic vinegar over the stuffed mushrooms just before serving for an extra burst of flavor. Garnish with additional fresh herbs if you like.

Serve these stuffed Portobello mushrooms as a hearty appetizer or a satisfying main dish. Enjoy!

Lobster Mac and Cheese

Ingredients

For the Mac and Cheese:

- **1 pound elbow macaroni** (or cavatappi, shells, etc.)
- **4 tablespoons unsalted butter**
- **1/4 cup all-purpose flour**
- **2 cups whole milk**
- **1 cup heavy cream**
- **2 cups sharp cheddar cheese**, shredded
- **1 cup Gruyère cheese**, shredded
- **1/2 cup Parmesan cheese**, grated
- **1/2 teaspoon Dijon mustard**
- **1/4 teaspoon paprika**
- **1/4 teaspoon garlic powder**
- **1/4 teaspoon onion powder**
- **Salt and black pepper to taste**

For the Lobster:

- **1 pound lobster meat**, cooked and chopped (fresh or thawed from frozen)
- **2 tablespoons unsalted butter**
- **1 tablespoon lemon juice**
- **1 tablespoon fresh parsley**, chopped (optional for garnish)

For the Topping:

- **1/2 cup panko breadcrumbs**
- **2 tablespoons unsalted butter**, melted
- **1/4 cup Parmesan cheese**, grated

Instructions

1. **Preheat Oven:**
   - Preheat your oven to 375°F (190°C).
2. **Cook the Pasta:**
   - Cook the macaroni according to package instructions until al dente. Drain and set aside.
3. **Prepare the Cheese Sauce:**
   - In a large saucepan, melt 4 tablespoons of butter over medium heat. Whisk in the flour and cook for about 1 minute, or until it forms a roux and starts to bubble.
   - Gradually whisk in the milk and heavy cream, continuing to stir until the mixture is smooth and begins to thicken.

- Add the shredded cheddar, Gruyère, and Parmesan cheeses. Stir until the cheese is fully melted and the sauce is smooth. Season with Dijon mustard, paprika, garlic powder, onion powder, salt, and black pepper.
4. **Prepare the Lobster:**
   - In a skillet, melt 2 tablespoons of butter over medium heat. Add the chopped lobster meat and cook for 2-3 minutes until heated through. Stir in the lemon juice and remove from heat.
5. **Combine Pasta and Sauce:**
   - Add the cooked macaroni and lobster to the cheese sauce. Stir until everything is well combined and evenly coated with the sauce.
6. **Transfer to Baking Dish:**
   - Pour the mac and cheese mixture into a greased 9x13-inch baking dish or a similarly sized oven-proof dish.
7. **Prepare the Topping:**
   - In a small bowl, mix together the panko breadcrumbs, melted butter, and Parmesan cheese. Sprinkle this mixture evenly over the top of the mac and cheese.
8. **Bake:**
   - Bake in the preheated oven for 25-30 minutes, or until the top is golden brown and the mac and cheese is bubbly.
9. **Garnish and Serve:**
   - If desired, garnish with fresh parsley before serving.

Enjoy your luxurious lobster mac and cheese, perfect for special occasions or a decadent treat!

Chicken Marsala

Ingredients

- 4 boneless, skinless chicken breasts
- 1/2 cup all-purpose flour
- Salt and black pepper to taste
- 2 tablespoons olive oil
- 4 tablespoons unsalted butter
- 1 cup Marsala wine
- 1 cup chicken broth
- 1 cup mushrooms, sliced (cremini or button mushrooms work well)
- 2 cloves garlic, minced
- 1 tablespoon fresh parsley, chopped (optional for garnish)

Instructions

1. **Prepare the Chicken:**
   - Place each chicken breast between two sheets of plastic wrap or parchment paper. Gently pound with a meat mallet or rolling pin to an even thickness, about 1/2 inch thick.
   - Season both sides of the chicken breasts with salt and black pepper. Dredge the chicken in flour, shaking off the excess.
2. **Cook the Chicken:**
   - Heat the olive oil in a large skillet over medium-high heat. Add 2 tablespoons of butter and let it melt.
   - Add the chicken breasts to the skillet and cook for about 4-5 minutes per side, or until golden brown and cooked through. Remove the chicken from the skillet and set aside on a plate.
3. **Prepare the Sauce:**
   - In the same skillet, add the remaining 2 tablespoons of butter. Add the sliced mushrooms and cook for 4-5 minutes, or until they are browned and tender.
   - Add the minced garlic and cook for 1 minute until fragrant.
4. **Deglaze the Pan:**
   - Pour in the Marsala wine, scraping up any browned bits from the bottom of the skillet. Let it simmer for 2-3 minutes to reduce slightly.
5. **Add Broth and Finish Sauce:**
   - Stir in the chicken broth and let the sauce simmer for another 3-4 minutes until it reduces and thickens slightly.
6. **Return Chicken to Skillet:**
   - Return the cooked chicken breasts to the skillet, spooning some of the sauce and mushrooms over the top. Simmer for another 2-3 minutes to reheat the chicken and allow it to absorb some of the sauce flavors.
7. **Serve:**

- Garnish with fresh chopped parsley if desired. Serve the Chicken Marsala with the mushroom sauce spooned over the top. It pairs well with mashed potatoes, rice, or pasta.

Enjoy your savory and delicious Chicken Marsala!

Beef Wellington

Ingredients

- **1 (2-3 pound) center-cut beef tenderloin**, trimmed
- **Salt and black pepper to taste**
- **2 tablespoons olive oil**
- **2 tablespoons Dijon mustard**
- **8 ounces cremini or button mushrooms**, finely chopped
- **2 tablespoons unsalted butter**
- **2 cloves garlic**, minced
- **1 small shallot**, finely chopped
- **1/4 cup dry white wine** (optional)
- **1 tablespoon fresh thyme leaves**
- **Puff pastry sheets** (enough to wrap the tenderloin completely, usually about 2 sheets)
- **8 slices prosciutto**
- **1 egg**, beaten (for egg wash)

Instructions

1. **Prepare the Beef Tenderloin:**
   - Season the beef tenderloin generously with salt and black pepper.
   - Heat olive oil in a large skillet over high heat. Sear the beef on all sides until browned, about 2-3 minutes per side. Remove from heat and let it cool. Brush the seared beef with Dijon mustard.
2. **Prepare the Mushroom Duxelles:**
   - In the same skillet, melt the butter over medium heat. Add the shallots and garlic, cooking until translucent, about 2 minutes.
   - Add the finely chopped mushrooms and cook until the moisture evaporates and the mushrooms start to brown, about 10 minutes. Stir in the white wine (if using) and cook until the liquid evaporates. Add the thyme leaves and season with salt and black pepper. Cool completely.
3. **Assemble the Wellington:**
   - Lay out the prosciutto slices on a piece of plastic wrap, slightly overlapping them. Spread the cooled mushroom duxelles evenly over the prosciutto.
   - Place the beef tenderloin on top of the mushroom mixture. Using the plastic wrap, roll the prosciutto and mushroom mixture around the beef, ensuring it's wrapped tightly. Chill in the refrigerator for 15 minutes to firm up.
4. **Wrap in Puff Pastry:**
   - Roll out the puff pastry sheets on a lightly floured surface. Place the wrapped beef (with the prosciutto and mushroom layer) in the center of the puff pastry. Fold the pastry over the beef, sealing the edges. Trim any excess pastry.
   - Place the wrapped beef seam-side down on a baking sheet lined with parchment paper. Brush the pastry with the beaten egg.
5. **Bake:**

        - Preheat your oven to 400°F (200°C).
        - Bake the Beef Wellington in the preheated oven for 25-30 minutes, or until the pastry is golden brown and the internal temperature of the beef reaches 125°F (52°C) for medium-rare. Use a meat thermometer to ensure accuracy.
6. **Rest and Serve:**
        - Let the Beef Wellington rest for 10 minutes before slicing. This helps the juices redistribute and makes slicing easier.

Enjoy your luxurious Beef Wellington with your favorite sides and sauces!

Butternut Squash Risotto

Ingredients

- **1 medium butternut squash**, peeled, seeded, and cut into 1/2-inch cubes
- **2 tablespoons olive oil**
- **1 small onion**, finely chopped
- **2 cloves garlic**, minced
- **1 1/2 cups Arborio rice**
- **1/2 cup dry white wine**
- **4 cups chicken or vegetable broth**, kept warm
- **1/2 cup grated Parmesan cheese**
- **2 tablespoons unsalted butter**
- **1/4 teaspoon ground nutmeg** (optional)
- **Salt and black pepper to taste**
- **2 tablespoons fresh sage leaves**, chopped (or 1 tablespoon dried sage)

Instructions

1. **Roast the Butternut Squash:**
   - Preheat your oven to 400°F (200°C).
   - Toss the butternut squash cubes with 1 tablespoon of olive oil and a pinch of salt and pepper. Spread the squash in a single layer on a baking sheet.
   - Roast for 25-30 minutes, or until the squash is tender and caramelized, stirring halfway through. Let it cool slightly, then mash with a fork or potato masher, leaving some chunks for texture.
2. **Prepare the Risotto Base:**
   - In a large skillet or saucepan, heat the remaining 1 tablespoon of olive oil over medium heat. Add the chopped onion and cook until translucent, about 5 minutes.
   - Stir in the minced garlic and cook for another 1 minute until fragrant.
3. **Cook the Risotto:**
   - Add the Arborio rice to the skillet and cook for 2 minutes, stirring constantly, until the rice is lightly toasted.
   - Pour in the white wine and stir until it has mostly evaporated.
   - Begin adding the warm broth, 1/2 cup at a time, stirring constantly. Allow the rice to absorb most of the liquid before adding more broth. This process should take about 18-20 minutes, and the rice should be creamy and tender but still have a slight bite.
4. **Add the Butternut Squash:**
   - Stir in the mashed butternut squash, Parmesan cheese, and butter. Continue stirring until the cheese and butter are melted and the risotto is creamy. Season with salt, black pepper, and ground nutmeg if using.
5. **Finish and Serve:**

- Stir in the fresh sage leaves and cook for another minute. Adjust seasoning as needed.
- Serve the risotto immediately, garnished with additional Parmesan cheese and sage if desired.

Enjoy your creamy and flavorful butternut squash risotto!

Mediterranean Stuffed Bell Peppers

Ingredients

- **4 large bell peppers** (any color)
- **1 cup cooked quinoa** (or couscous)
- **1/2 cup feta cheese**, crumbled
- **1/2 cup Kalamata olives**, pitted and chopped
- **1/2 cup cherry tomatoes**, halved
- **1/4 cup red onion**, finely chopped
- **1/4 cup fresh parsley**, chopped
- **2 cloves garlic**, minced
- **1 teaspoon dried oregano**
- **1/2 teaspoon dried basil**
- **1/4 teaspoon ground cumin**
- **Salt and black pepper to taste**
- **2 tablespoons olive oil**
- **1 tablespoon lemon juice**

Instructions

1. **Preheat Oven:**
    - Preheat your oven to 375°F (190°C).
2. **Prepare the Bell Peppers:**
    - Cut the tops off the bell peppers and remove the seeds and membranes. Set aside.
3. **Prepare the Filling:**
    - In a large bowl, combine the cooked quinoa, crumbled feta cheese, chopped olives, cherry tomatoes, red onion, parsley, minced garlic, dried oregano, dried basil, ground cumin, salt, and black pepper.
    - Drizzle with olive oil and lemon juice. Toss everything together until well mixed.
4. **Stuff the Peppers:**
    - Spoon the quinoa mixture into each bell pepper, packing it gently to fill them completely.
5. **Bake:**
    - Place the stuffed peppers upright in a baking dish. Cover the dish with aluminum foil.
    - Bake in the preheated oven for 30 minutes. Remove the foil and bake for an additional 10 minutes, or until the peppers are tender and slightly charred on top.
6. **Serve:**
    - Let the stuffed peppers cool for a few minutes before serving. They can be served warm or at room temperature.

Enjoy your Mediterranean stuffed bell peppers, packed with flavor and nutrients!

Lobster Tail with Lemon Butter

Ingredients

- **4 lobster tails** (about 6-8 ounces each)
- **1/2 cup unsalted butter**, melted
- **2 tablespoons fresh lemon juice**
- **2 cloves garlic**, minced
- **1 teaspoon fresh parsley**, chopped (or 1/2 teaspoon dried parsley)
- **1/2 teaspoon paprika**
- **1/4 teaspoon cayenne pepper** (optional, for a bit of heat)
- **Salt and black pepper to taste**
- **Lemon wedges** (for serving)

Instructions

1. **Prepare the Lobster Tails:**
    - Preheat your oven to 425°F (220°C).
    - Using kitchen scissors or a sharp knife, cut the top shell of each lobster tail lengthwise down the center. Be careful not to cut into the meat. Gently pull apart the shell to expose the meat. You can also lift the meat slightly out of the shell for easier eating.
2. **Prepare the Lemon Butter:**
    - In a small bowl, mix together the melted butter, lemon juice, minced garlic, parsley, paprika, cayenne pepper (if using), salt, and black pepper.
3. **Apply the Butter:**
    - Brush the lobster meat generously with the lemon butter mixture, making sure to get some of the butter into the crevices.
4. **Bake the Lobster:**
    - Place the prepared lobster tails on a baking sheet. Bake in the preheated oven for 10-12 minutes, or until the lobster meat is opaque and cooked through. The internal temperature should reach 140°F (60°C).
5. **Broil (Optional):**
    - For a slightly crispy top, you can broil the lobster tails for an additional 2-3 minutes after baking. Keep a close eye on them to avoid burning.
6. **Serve:**
    - Brush the lobster tails with any remaining lemon butter and serve with lemon wedges on the side for extra zest.

Enjoy your delicious lobster tails with a rich lemon butter sauce!

Cranberry Orange Glazed Pork

Ingredients

For the Pork:

- 2 pounds pork tenderloin
- 2 tablespoons olive oil
- Salt and black pepper to taste

For the Cranberry Orange Glaze:

- 1 cup cranberry sauce (store-bought or homemade)
- 1/4 cup orange juice
- 2 tablespoons orange zest
- 1 tablespoon Dijon mustard
- 2 tablespoons honey
- 1 tablespoon soy sauce
- 1/2 teaspoon ground cinnamon
- 1/4 teaspoon ground cloves

Instructions

1. **Prepare the Pork Tenderloin:**
    - Preheat your oven to 400°F (200°C).
    - Pat the pork tenderloin dry with paper towels. Season generously with salt and black pepper.
    - Heat the olive oil in an oven-proof skillet over medium-high heat. Sear the pork tenderloin on all sides until browned, about 2-3 minutes per side.
2. **Prepare the Glaze:**
    - In a medium saucepan, combine the cranberry sauce, orange juice, orange zest, Dijon mustard, honey, soy sauce, ground cinnamon, and ground cloves. Stir to combine and bring to a simmer over medium heat. Cook for 5-7 minutes until the glaze thickens slightly.
3. **Glaze the Pork:**
    - Brush the seared pork tenderloin generously with the cranberry orange glaze. Reserve some glaze for serving.
4. **Roast the Pork:**
    - Transfer the skillet with the glazed pork tenderloin to the preheated oven. Roast for 20-25 minutes, or until the internal temperature of the pork reaches 145°F (63°C). Baste with additional glaze halfway through cooking.
5. **Rest and Slice:**
    - Remove the pork tenderloin from the oven and let it rest for 10 minutes before slicing. This helps the juices redistribute and makes the pork tender.
6. **Serve:**

- Slice the pork tenderloin and serve with the remaining cranberry orange glaze drizzled over the top. This dish pairs well with roasted vegetables, mashed potatoes, or a simple salad.

Enjoy your flavorful and festive cranberry orange glazed pork!

Teriyaki Glazed Salmon

Ingredients

For the Teriyaki Glaze:

- **1/2 cup soy sauce**
- **1/4 cup honey**
- **1/4 cup mirin** (Japanese sweet rice wine) or dry white wine
- **2 tablespoons rice vinegar**
- **2 tablespoons brown sugar**
- **2 cloves garlic**, minced
- **1 teaspoon fresh ginger**, minced
- **1 teaspoon cornstarch** (optional, for thickening)
- **1 tablespoon water** (if using cornstarch)

For the Salmon:

- **4 salmon fillets** (about 6 ounces each)
- **1 tablespoon olive oil**
- **Salt and black pepper to taste**
- **Sesame seeds** (for garnish, optional)
- **Chopped green onions** (for garnish, optional)
- **Lime wedges** (for serving, optional)

Instructions

1. **Prepare the Teriyaki Glaze:**
   - In a small saucepan, combine the soy sauce, honey, mirin, rice vinegar, brown sugar, minced garlic, and minced ginger.
   - Bring to a simmer over medium heat, stirring occasionally. Simmer for 5-7 minutes until the glaze thickens slightly. If you prefer a thicker glaze, mix the cornstarch with water to make a slurry and stir it into the glaze. Simmer for an additional 1-2 minutes until thickened. Remove from heat and set aside.
2. **Prepare the Salmon:**
   - Preheat your oven to 400°F (200°C) or preheat your grill to medium-high heat.
   - Pat the salmon fillets dry with paper towels. Brush lightly with olive oil and season with salt and black pepper.
3. **Cook the Salmon:**
   - **Oven Method:** Place the salmon fillets on a baking sheet lined with parchment paper or lightly greased. Bake for 12-15 minutes, or until the salmon flakes easily with a fork and reaches an internal temperature of 145°F (63°C).
   - **Grill Method:** Place the salmon fillets on the grill, skin-side down. Grill for 4-5 minutes per side, or until the salmon is cooked through and flakes easily with a fork.

4. **Glaze the Salmon:**
   - During the last 2-3 minutes of cooking, brush the salmon fillets generously with the teriyaki glaze. If you prefer, you can also glaze the salmon after removing it from the heat.
5. **Serve:**
   - Remove the salmon from the oven or grill and let it rest for a couple of minutes.
   - Garnish with sesame seeds and chopped green onions if desired. Serve with lime wedges and additional teriyaki glaze on the side.

Enjoy your delicious teriyaki glazed salmon with rice, steamed vegetables, or a fresh salad!

Spinach and Artichoke Stuffed Chicken

Ingredients

- **4 boneless, skinless chicken breasts**
- **1 cup fresh spinach**, chopped
- **1 cup marinated artichoke hearts**, chopped
- **1/2 cup cream cheese**, softened
- **1/2 cup grated Parmesan cheese**
- **1/4 cup shredded mozzarella cheese**
- **2 cloves garlic**, minced
- **1 tablespoon olive oil**
- **1/2 teaspoon dried oregano**
- **1/2 teaspoon dried basil**
- **Salt and black pepper to taste**
- **Toothpicks** or kitchen twine

Instructions

1. **Prepare the Filling:**
    - In a medium bowl, mix together the chopped spinach, chopped artichoke hearts, cream cheese, Parmesan cheese, mozzarella cheese, and minced garlic. Season with salt, black pepper, dried oregano, and dried basil. Stir until well combined.
2. **Prepare the Chicken:**
    - Preheat your oven to 375°F (190°C).
    - Place each chicken breast between two sheets of plastic wrap or parchment paper. Gently pound with a meat mallet or rolling pin until the breasts are an even thickness, about 1/2 inch thick.
    - Season both sides of the chicken breasts with salt and black pepper.
3. **Stuff the Chicken:**
    - Spoon a generous amount of the spinach and artichoke filling onto one side of each chicken breast. Fold the other side of the chicken over the filling and secure with toothpicks or kitchen twine. Repeat with the remaining chicken breasts.
4. **Sear the Chicken:**
    - Heat olive oil in a large oven-proof skillet over medium-high heat. Add the stuffed chicken breasts and cook for 2-3 minutes per side, or until golden brown. This step helps to seal in the juices and adds a nice color.
5. **Bake the Chicken:**
    - Transfer the skillet to the preheated oven. Bake for 20-25 minutes, or until the chicken is cooked through and the internal temperature reaches 165°F (74°C). Remove from the oven and let the chicken rest for 5 minutes.
6. **Serve:**
    - Carefully remove the toothpicks or twine from the chicken breasts. Slice and serve hot, garnished with additional Parmesan cheese or fresh herbs if desired.

Enjoy your flavorful and creamy spinach and artichoke stuffed chicken! It pairs wonderfully with a side of roasted vegetables, rice, or a fresh salad.

Garlic Butter Shrimp

Ingredients

- **1 pound large shrimp**, peeled and deveined
- **4 tablespoons unsalted butter**
- **2 tablespoons olive oil**
- **4 cloves garlic**, minced
- **1/4 teaspoon red pepper flakes** (optional, for a bit of heat)
- **1 tablespoon fresh lemon juice**
- **1/4 cup fresh parsley**, chopped
- **Salt and black pepper to taste**
- **Lemon wedges** (for serving, optional)

Instructions

1. **Prepare the Shrimp:**
   - Pat the shrimp dry with paper towels and season with a pinch of salt and black pepper.
2. **Cook the Shrimp:**
   - Heat the olive oil and 2 tablespoons of butter in a large skillet over medium-high heat.
   - Add the shrimp in a single layer and cook for about 2-3 minutes on each side, or until they turn pink and opaque. Be careful not to overcook them. Remove the shrimp from the skillet and set aside.
3. **Prepare the Garlic Butter Sauce:**
   - In the same skillet, reduce the heat to medium. Add the remaining 2 tablespoons of butter.
   - Once the butter is melted, add the minced garlic and red pepper flakes (if using). Sauté for about 1 minute, or until the garlic is fragrant but not browned.
4. **Combine and Finish:**
   - Return the cooked shrimp to the skillet and toss to coat in the garlic butter sauce. Cook for an additional 1-2 minutes, just until the shrimp are heated through and well coated.
   - Stir in the fresh lemon juice and chopped parsley. Adjust seasoning with more salt and black pepper if needed.
5. **Serve:**
   - Serve the garlic butter shrimp immediately with lemon wedges on the side if desired. This dish pairs well with pasta, rice, or a fresh salad.

Enjoy your succulent and flavorful garlic butter shrimp!

Beef Stroganoff

Ingredients

- **1 pound beef sirloin or tenderloin**, thinly sliced into strips
- **2 tablespoons olive oil**
- **1 small onion**, finely chopped
- **2 cloves garlic**, minced
- **8 ounces cremini or button mushrooms**, sliced
- **1 tablespoon all-purpose flour**
- **1 cup beef broth**
- **1 cup sour cream**
- **1 tablespoon Dijon mustard**
- **1 teaspoon Worcestershire sauce**
- **1/2 teaspoon paprika**
- **Salt and black pepper to taste**
- **2 tablespoons fresh parsley**, chopped (for garnish)
- **Egg noodles** or **rice** (for serving)

Instructions

1. **Prepare the Beef:**
   - Season the beef strips with salt and black pepper.
2. **Brown the Beef:**
   - Heat the olive oil in a large skillet or sauté pan over medium-high heat. Add the beef strips in batches (to avoid overcrowding) and cook until browned on all sides, about 2-3 minutes per side. Remove the beef from the skillet and set aside.
3. **Cook the Vegetables:**
   - In the same skillet, add the chopped onion and cook until softened, about 3 minutes. Add the minced garlic and cook for an additional 1 minute until fragrant.
   - Add the sliced mushrooms and cook until they release their moisture and become golden brown, about 5-7 minutes.
4. **Make the Sauce:**
   - Sprinkle the flour over the mushrooms and onions, and stir to combine. Cook for 1 minute to remove the raw flour taste.
   - Gradually add the beef broth, stirring constantly to prevent lumps. Bring the mixture to a simmer and cook until the sauce begins to thicken, about 3-4 minutes.
5. **Finish the Stroganoff:**
   - Return the browned beef to the skillet and stir to combine with the sauce. Cook for another 2-3 minutes to heat the beef through.
   - Reduce the heat to low and stir in the sour cream, Dijon mustard, Worcestershire sauce, and paprika. Cook gently until the sauce is creamy and heated through. Adjust seasoning with salt and black pepper.

6. **Serve:**
    - Serve the beef stroganoff over cooked egg noodles or rice. Garnish with fresh parsley.

Enjoy your hearty and creamy beef stroganoff!

Creamy Mushroom Soup

Ingredients

- **1 lb (450g) fresh mushrooms** (button, cremini, or a mix), sliced
- **1 medium onion**, finely chopped
- **3 cloves garlic**, minced
- **3 tbsp unsalted butter**
- **2 tbsp olive oil**
- **4 cups (1 liter) chicken or vegetable broth**
- **1 cup (240ml) heavy cream**
- **1/4 cup (60ml) dry white wine** (optional)
- **1 tbsp all-purpose flour**
- **Salt and black pepper**, to taste
- **1 tsp dried thyme** or **1 tbsp fresh thyme**, chopped
- **1 bay leaf**
- **Fresh parsley or chives**, for garnish (optional)

Instructions

1. **Prepare the Mushrooms**: Clean and slice the mushrooms. If using a mix of mushrooms, try to chop them into similar-sized pieces for even cooking.
2. **Sauté Vegetables**: In a large pot or Dutch oven, heat the butter and olive oil over medium heat. Add the chopped onions and cook until softened and translucent, about 5 minutes.
3. **Cook Garlic and Mushrooms**: Add the minced garlic and cook for an additional minute. Then add the sliced mushrooms and cook until they release their moisture and become golden brown, about 8-10 minutes. Stir occasionally.
4. **Add Flour**: Sprinkle the flour over the mushrooms and stir to coat. Cook for another 2 minutes to remove the raw flour taste.
5. **Deglaze**: If using white wine, pour it in now and stir, scraping up any brown bits from the bottom of the pot. Allow the wine to reduce for about 2 minutes.
6. **Add Broth and Seasonings**: Pour in the chicken or vegetable broth, add the bay leaf, thyme, and season with salt and black pepper. Bring the mixture to a boil, then reduce the heat and simmer for about 15 minutes.
7. **Blend the Soup**: Remove the bay leaf. Use an immersion blender to blend the soup until smooth, or carefully transfer the soup to a blender in batches and blend. If you prefer a chunkier texture, blend only half of the soup.
8. **Finish with Cream**: Return the blended soup to the pot (if needed) and stir in the heavy cream. Heat through, but do not boil. Adjust seasoning to taste.
9. **Serve**: Ladle the soup into bowls and garnish with chopped parsley or chives if desired. Serve hot with crusty bread or a side salad.

Enjoy your creamy mushroom soup! It's rich, flavorful, and perfect for any occasion.

Maple Glazed Carrots

Ingredients

- **1 lb (450g) baby carrots** (or regular carrots, peeled and cut into sticks)
- **2 tbsp unsalted butter**
- **1/4 cup pure maple syrup**
- **1 tbsp brown sugar** (optional, for extra sweetness)
- **1/2 tsp ground cinnamon** (optional, for added warmth)
- **1/4 tsp salt**
- **1/4 tsp black pepper**
- **1/4 cup water**
- **1 tbsp chopped fresh parsley** (optional, for garnish)

Instructions

1. **Prepare Carrots**: If using regular carrots, peel and cut them into sticks. If using baby carrots, just trim the ends.
2. **Cook Carrots**: In a large skillet or sauté pan, melt the butter over medium heat. Add the carrots and cook for about 5 minutes, stirring occasionally, until they start to soften.
3. **Add Syrup and Seasonings**: Stir in the maple syrup, brown sugar (if using), cinnamon (if using), salt, and pepper. Add the water and bring the mixture to a simmer.
4. **Glaze Carrots**: Reduce the heat to medium-low and cook, stirring occasionally, until the carrots are tender and the syrup has thickened into a glaze, about 10-15 minutes. If the glaze gets too thick before the carrots are done, add a little more water as needed.
5. **Finish and Serve**: Once the carrots are tender and nicely glazed, remove from heat. Garnish with chopped fresh parsley if desired.

These maple glazed carrots are sweet, savory, and have a lovely caramelized finish. They make a perfect side dish for a variety of meals, from weeknight dinners to holiday feasts. Enjoy!

Roasted Brussels Sprouts with Bacon

Ingredients

- **1 lb (450g) Brussels sprouts**, trimmed and halved
- **4-6 slices bacon**, cut into small pieces
- **2 tbsp olive oil**
- **1/2 tsp garlic powder**
- **1/2 tsp onion powder**
- **Salt and black pepper**, to taste
- **1/4 cup grated Parmesan cheese** (optional, for extra flavor)
- **1 tbsp balsamic vinegar** (optional, for a tangy finish)
- **Chopped fresh parsley** (optional, for garnish)

Instructions

1. **Preheat Oven**: Preheat your oven to 400°F (200°C).
2. **Prepare Bacon**: In a large bowl, toss the bacon pieces with a little bit of the olive oil to coat. Spread the bacon out on a baking sheet lined with parchment paper or aluminum foil.
3. **Cook Bacon**: Roast the bacon in the preheated oven for about 10-12 minutes, or until crispy. Remove from the oven and set aside, leaving the rendered bacon fat on the baking sheet.
4. **Prepare Brussels Sprouts**: While the bacon is cooking, trim the Brussels sprouts and cut them in half. In a large bowl, toss the Brussels sprouts with the remaining olive oil, garlic powder, onion powder, salt, and black pepper.
5. **Roast Brussels Sprouts**: After removing the bacon, spread the seasoned Brussels sprouts on the same baking sheet with the bacon fat. Roast in the oven for about 20-25 minutes, or until the sprouts are golden brown and crispy on the edges. Toss halfway through cooking for even roasting.
6. **Combine**: Once the Brussels sprouts are done, remove them from the oven. Toss them with the cooked bacon pieces and, if using, the Parmesan cheese and balsamic vinegar.
7. **Serve**: Garnish with chopped fresh parsley if desired. Serve immediately while hot.

This dish is perfect for adding a savory touch to any meal and is especially popular for holiday dinners or as a hearty side for weeknight meals. Enjoy!

Parmesan Crusted Chicken

Ingredients

- 4 boneless, skinless chicken breasts
- 1 cup grated Parmesan cheese
- 1 cup panko breadcrumbs
- 1/2 cup all-purpose flour
- 2 large eggs
- 1/4 cup milk
- **2 cloves garlic**, minced
- 1 tsp dried oregano
- 1 tsp dried basil
- **Salt and black pepper**, to taste
- 2 tbsp olive oil
- **Fresh parsley or basil**, for garnish (optional)

Instructions

1. **Prepare Chicken**: Preheat your oven to 400°F (200°C). If the chicken breasts are very thick, you might want to pound them to an even thickness using a meat mallet or rolling pin. This ensures they cook evenly.
2. **Prepare Breading Stations**: Set up a breading station with three shallow dishes:
    - In the first dish, place the flour.
    - In the second dish, whisk together the eggs and milk.
    - In the third dish, combine the grated Parmesan cheese, panko breadcrumbs, minced garlic, dried oregano, dried basil, salt, and pepper.
3. **Bread the Chicken**:
    - Dredge each chicken breast in the flour, shaking off any excess.
    - Dip it into the egg mixture, allowing any excess to drip off.
    - Press the chicken into the Parmesan-breadcrumb mixture, coating it evenly and pressing gently to help the coating adhere.
4. **Cook Chicken**:
    - Heat the olive oil in a large oven-safe skillet over medium-high heat.
    - Add the coated chicken breasts and cook for 2-3 minutes on each side, or until the coating is golden brown. This step helps to get the crust crispy.
    - Transfer the skillet to the preheated oven and bake for 15-20 minutes, or until the chicken reaches an internal temperature of 165°F (74°C) and is cooked through.
5. **Serve**: Remove from the oven and let the chicken rest for a few minutes before slicing. Garnish with chopped fresh parsley or basil if desired.

Tips

- **Make It Extra Crispy**: For an even crispier crust, you can add a bit of grated Parmesan cheese directly to the breadcrumbs or use a combination of regular and panko breadcrumbs.
- **Add Flavor Variations**: Feel free to add other seasonings to the breadcrumb mixture, like paprika, cayenne pepper, or Italian seasoning for a different twist.
- **Serve With**: This chicken pairs beautifully with a side of roasted vegetables, a fresh salad, or over pasta for a complete meal.

Enjoy your Parmesan crusted chicken! It's sure to be a hit with its irresistible, crunchy coating and cheesy goodness.

Creamy Spinach and Ricotta Stuffed Shells

Ingredients

- **20-24 jumbo pasta shells**
- **2 cups ricotta cheese**
- **1 cup grated Parmesan cheese**
- **1 cup shredded mozzarella cheese**
- **1 large egg**
- **2 cups fresh spinach**, chopped
- **2 cloves garlic**, minced
- **1/2 tsp dried oregano**
- **1/2 tsp dried basil**
- **Salt and black pepper**, to taste
- **2 cups marinara sauce** (store-bought or homemade)
- **1/2 cup grated Parmesan cheese** (for topping)
- **Fresh basil or parsley**, for garnish (optional)

Instructions

1. **Cook Pasta Shells**: Preheat your oven to 375°F (190°C). Cook the jumbo pasta shells according to the package instructions until al dente. Drain and let cool slightly.
2. **Prepare Filling**:
    - In a large bowl, mix together the ricotta cheese, 1 cup grated Parmesan cheese, 1 cup shredded mozzarella cheese, and egg.
    - Add the chopped spinach, minced garlic, dried oregano, dried basil, salt, and pepper. Mix until well combined.
3. **Prepare Marinara Sauce**: Spread a thin layer of marinara sauce on the bottom of a baking dish (about 9x13 inches).
4. **Stuff the Shells**: Spoon the spinach and ricotta mixture into each cooked shell. Place the stuffed shells seam-side up in the baking dish over the marinara sauce.
5. **Top with Sauce and Cheese**: Once all the shells are stuffed and in the dish, pour the remaining marinara sauce over the shells. Sprinkle the top with 1/2 cup grated Parmesan cheese and additional shredded mozzarella if desired.
6. **Bake**: Cover the baking dish with aluminum foil and bake in the preheated oven for 25 minutes. Remove the foil and bake for an additional 10-15 minutes, or until the cheese is bubbly and golden.
7. **Garnish and Serve**: Let the dish cool slightly before serving. Garnish with fresh basil or parsley if desired.

Tips

- **For Extra Flavor**: Sauté the spinach with a bit of olive oil and garlic before adding it to the cheese mixture. This adds depth to the filling.

- **Make Ahead**: You can assemble the stuffed shells a day in advance and refrigerate them until ready to bake. Just add a few extra minutes to the baking time if cooking from cold.
- **Freezing**: To freeze, assemble the shells and sauce in a baking dish, cover tightly with plastic wrap and foil, and freeze for up to 3 months. Bake directly from frozen, adding additional time as needed.

These creamy spinach and ricotta stuffed shells are a hearty and satisfying meal that pairs wonderfully with a side salad and some crusty garlic bread. Enjoy your delicious, comforting dinner!

Balsamic Glazed Steak

Ingredients

- **4 boneless ribeye steaks** (or your preferred cut)
- **Salt and black pepper**, to taste
- **2 tbsp olive oil**
- **1/2 cup balsamic vinegar**
- **1/4 cup honey**
- **2 cloves garlic**, minced
- **1 tbsp Dijon mustard**
- **1 tsp fresh rosemary** or **thyme**, finely chopped (optional)
- **1 tbsp butter** (optional, for added richness)
- **Fresh rosemary** or **thyme**, for garnish (optional)

Instructions

1. **Season the Steaks**: Season both sides of the steaks generously with salt and black pepper.
2. **Prepare the Glaze**: In a small saucepan, combine the balsamic vinegar, honey, minced garlic, and Dijon mustard. Bring the mixture to a simmer over medium heat, stirring occasionally.
3. **Reduce the Glaze**: Let the mixture simmer for about 5-7 minutes, or until it has reduced by about half and thickened into a syrupy consistency. If using fresh herbs, stir them in during the last minute of simmering. Remove from heat and set aside.
4. **Cook the Steaks**:
    - Heat olive oil in a large skillet over medium-high heat.
    - Add the steaks to the hot skillet and cook for 4-5 minutes per side for medium-rare, or to your desired doneness. Adjust cooking times based on the thickness of the steaks and your preferred level of doneness.
    - For extra flavor and richness, you can add a tablespoon of butter to the pan during the last minute of cooking and spoon it over the steaks.
5. **Rest the Steaks**: Remove the steaks from the skillet and let them rest on a plate for 5 minutes before slicing. This allows the juices to redistribute.
6. **Glaze the Steaks**: Drizzle the balsamic glaze over the steaks just before serving.
7. **Garnish and Serve**: Garnish with additional fresh rosemary or thyme if desired, and serve with your favorite sides.

Tips

- **For Perfect Steaks**: Use a meat thermometer to ensure your steaks are cooked to your desired doneness. Aim for 130°F (54°C) for medium-rare, 140°F (60°C) for medium, and 150°F (66°C) for medium-well.

- **For a Richer Glaze**: If you prefer a richer glaze, add a bit of butter to the balsamic glaze after removing it from the heat and stir until melted.
- **Side Suggestions**: This steak pairs wonderfully with roasted vegetables, mashed potatoes, or a fresh salad.

Enjoy your balsamic glazed steak! It's a flavorful and elegant dish that's sure to impress.

Herb Roasted Turkey Breast

Ingredients

- **1 (3-4 lb or 1.4-1.8 kg) bone-in, skin-on turkey breast**
- **2 tbsp olive oil**
- **1 tbsp fresh rosemary**, chopped (or 1 tsp dried rosemary)
- **1 tbsp fresh thyme**, chopped (or 1 tsp dried thyme)
- **1 tbsp fresh sage**, chopped (or 1 tsp dried sage)
- **3 cloves garlic**, minced
- **1 lemon**, zested and juiced
- **Salt and black pepper**, to taste
- **1 cup chicken broth** (or white wine)
- **1 onion**, quartered
- **1-2 carrots**, cut into chunks
- **1-2 celery stalks**, cut into chunks

Instructions

1. **Preheat Oven**: Preheat your oven to 375°F (190°C).
2. **Prepare the Turkey Breast**:
    - Pat the turkey breast dry with paper towels.
    - Carefully loosen the skin from the meat by sliding your fingers between the skin and the breast meat, being careful not to tear the skin.
3. **Make Herb Mixture**:
    - In a small bowl, combine the olive oil, rosemary, thyme, sage, minced garlic, lemon zest, and lemon juice.
    - Season the mixture with salt and black pepper.
4. **Season the Turkey**:
    - Rub the herb mixture under the skin and over the surface of the turkey breast.
    - Season the outside of the turkey breast generously with salt and black pepper.
5. **Prepare the Roasting Pan**:
    - Place the onion, carrots, and celery in the bottom of a roasting pan to create a rack for the turkey breast. This will help flavor the turkey and keep it elevated.
6. **Roast the Turkey**:
    - Place the turkey breast on top of the vegetables in the roasting pan.
    - Pour the chicken broth (or white wine) into the bottom of the pan.
7. **Roast and Baste**:
    - Roast the turkey breast in the preheated oven for about 1.5 to 2 hours, or until the internal temperature reaches 165°F (74°C) and the skin is golden brown and crispy. Baste the turkey occasionally with the pan juices to keep it moist.
8. **Rest the Turkey**:
    - Remove the turkey breast from the oven and let it rest for 15-20 minutes before carving. This helps the juices redistribute and makes for a juicier turkey.

9. **Serve**:
    - Slice the turkey breast and serve with your favorite sides. You can also strain the pan juices to make a simple gravy if desired.

Tips

- **For Extra Crispy Skin**: If the skin isn't as crispy as you'd like, you can broil the turkey breast for a few minutes at the end of roasting, keeping a close eye on it to prevent burning.
- **For Even Cooking**: If the turkey breast is particularly large or uneven, you can truss it with kitchen twine to ensure even cooking.
- **Make Ahead**: You can prepare the herb mixture and season the turkey breast a day in advance. Keep it covered in the refrigerator until you're ready to roast.

This herb-roasted turkey breast is tender, flavorful, and perfect for a festive meal or a comforting dinner. Enjoy!

Lemon Herb Chicken Thighs

Ingredients

- **4 bone-in, skin-on chicken thighs**
- **2 tbsp olive oil**
- **1 lemon**, zested and juiced
- **3 cloves garlic**, minced
- **1 tbsp fresh rosemary**, chopped (or 1 tsp dried rosemary)
- **1 tbsp fresh thyme**, chopped (or 1 tsp dried thyme)
- **1 tsp dried oregano**
- **Salt and black pepper**, to taste
- **1/4 cup chicken broth** (optional, for a bit of moisture and flavor)
- **Lemon wedges**, for serving (optional)
- **Fresh parsley**, chopped, for garnish (optional)

Instructions

1. **Preheat Oven**: Preheat your oven to 400°F (200°C).
2. **Prepare Chicken Thighs**:
   - Pat the chicken thighs dry with paper towels to ensure crispy skin.
   - Season both sides of the chicken thighs generously with salt and black pepper.
3. **Make the Marinade**:
   - In a small bowl, combine the olive oil, lemon zest, lemon juice, minced garlic, rosemary, thyme, and oregano.
4. **Marinate the Chicken**:
   - Rub the marinade all over the chicken thighs, making sure to get some under the skin if possible.
   - Let the chicken marinate for at least 15 minutes, or up to 1 hour if you have more time. For even more flavor, marinate overnight in the refrigerator.
5. **Prepare the Baking Dish**:
   - Place the marinated chicken thighs in a baking dish or on a rimmed baking sheet. If using, pour the chicken broth into the bottom of the dish to help keep the chicken moist and add flavor.
6. **Roast the Chicken**:
   - Roast the chicken thighs in the preheated oven for about 35-45 minutes, or until the skin is crispy and the internal temperature reaches 165°F (74°C). The exact time will depend on the size of the thighs.
7. **Optional Broil**:
   - If you want extra crispy skin, you can broil the chicken for an additional 2-3 minutes at the end of cooking, but keep a close eye on it to avoid burning.
8. **Rest and Serve**:
   - Let the chicken thighs rest for about 5 minutes before serving to allow the juices to redistribute.

- Garnish with fresh parsley and lemon wedges if desired.

Tips

- **For Even Cooking**: Arrange the chicken thighs skin-side up in the baking dish so they cook evenly and the skin becomes crispy.
- **Add Vegetables**: You can add vegetables like potatoes, carrots, or bell peppers to the baking dish for a complete meal. Just toss them in a bit of olive oil and seasoning, and roast them alongside the chicken.
- **Use a Meat Thermometer**: For best results, use a meat thermometer to ensure the chicken is cooked through to the proper temperature.

This lemon herb chicken thighs recipe is fresh, flavorful, and perfect for a weeknight dinner or a special occasion. Enjoy your meal!

Truffle Mac and Cheese

Ingredients

For the Mac and Cheese:

- **8 oz (225g) elbow macaroni** (or your preferred pasta)
- **2 tbsp unsalted butter**
- **2 tbsp all-purpose flour**
- **2 cups whole milk**
- **1 cup heavy cream**
- **1 cup grated Gruyère cheese**
- **1 cup shredded sharp cheddar cheese**
- **1/2 cup grated Parmesan cheese**
- **2 tbsp truffle oil** (or more to taste)
- **1-2 tbsp black truffle paste** (optional, for extra truffle flavor)
- **Salt and black pepper**, to taste

For the Topping:

- **1 cup panko breadcrumbs**
- **2 tbsp unsalted butter**, melted
- **1/4 cup grated Parmesan cheese**
- **1 tbsp chopped fresh parsley** (optional, for garnish)

Instructions

1. **Cook the Pasta**: Preheat your oven to 375°F (190°C). Cook the macaroni according to package instructions until al dente. Drain and set aside.
2. **Prepare the Cheese Sauce**:
    - In a large saucepan, melt the butter over medium heat. Stir in the flour and cook, stirring constantly, for about 1-2 minutes until the mixture is lightly golden (this forms a roux).
    - Gradually whisk in the milk and heavy cream, and cook until the mixture starts to thicken and is smooth.
    - Reduce the heat to low and add the Gruyère, cheddar, and Parmesan cheeses, stirring until melted and smooth.
    - Stir in the truffle oil and truffle paste (if using). Season with salt and black pepper to taste.
3. **Combine Pasta and Sauce**: Fold the cooked macaroni into the cheese sauce, ensuring that all the pasta is well coated.
4. **Prepare the Topping**:
    - In a small bowl, combine the panko breadcrumbs, melted butter, and grated Parmesan cheese.
5. **Assemble and Bake**:

- Pour the mac and cheese into a baking dish (about 8x8 inches or similar).
- Sprinkle the breadcrumb mixture evenly over the top.
- Bake in the preheated oven for about 20-25 minutes, or until the top is golden brown and crispy.
6. **Garnish and Serve**:
    - Let the mac and cheese cool for a few minutes before serving.
    - Garnish with chopped fresh parsley if desired.

Tips

- **Adjust Truffle Flavor**: Start with 2 tablespoons of truffle oil and adjust to taste. If you love truffles, you can add more or use truffle salt for a different kind of truffle flavor.
- **For Extra Richness**: You can use a mix of different cheeses like fontina or Asiago for additional depth of flavor.
- **Make Ahead**: You can prepare the mac and cheese up to 2 days in advance. Just assemble it, cover it, and refrigerate. Bake it right before serving, adding a few extra minutes to the cooking time if needed.

This truffle mac and cheese is a luxurious treat that combines creamy, cheesy goodness with the unique and aromatic flavor of truffles. Enjoy!

Pomegranate Glazed Pork Chops

Ingredients

- **4 bone-in or boneless pork chops** (about 1-inch thick)
- **Salt and black pepper**, to taste
- **2 tbsp olive oil**
- **1 cup pomegranate juice**
- **1/4 cup honey**
- **2 tbsp balsamic vinegar**
- **1 clove garlic**, minced
- **1 tsp fresh rosemary** or **thyme**, chopped (optional)
- **1 tbsp cornstarch** (optional, for thickening)
- **1 tbsp water** (optional, for thickening)
- **Pomegranate seeds** (optional, for garnish)
- **Fresh rosemary** or **thyme**, for garnish (optional)

Instructions

1. **Season the Pork Chops**:
   - Pat the pork chops dry with paper towels.
   - Season both sides generously with salt and black pepper.
2. **Cook the Pork Chops**:
   - Heat olive oil in a large skillet over medium-high heat.
   - Add the pork chops and cook for about 4-5 minutes on each side, or until the internal temperature reaches 145°F (63°C) and the pork chops are golden brown and cooked through. Remove the pork chops from the skillet and set aside on a plate.
3. **Prepare the Pomegranate Glaze**:
   - In the same skillet, reduce the heat to medium.
   - Add the pomegranate juice, honey, balsamic vinegar, minced garlic, and fresh herbs (if using). Stir to combine.
   - Simmer the mixture for about 10-15 minutes, or until it has reduced by half and thickened slightly. If you want a thicker glaze, mix cornstarch with water to make a slurry and stir it into the glaze. Continue to cook for an additional 1-2 minutes until thickened.
4. **Glaze the Pork Chops**:
   - Return the pork chops to the skillet, spooning some of the glaze over them. Cook for an additional 2-3 minutes, allowing the pork chops to heat through and absorb some of the glaze.
5. **Serve**:
   - Transfer the pork chops to serving plates and spoon the remaining glaze over them.
   - Garnish with pomegranate seeds and fresh rosemary or thyme if desired.

Tips

- **For Extra Flavor**: You can marinate the pork chops in a mixture of olive oil, garlic, and herbs for a few hours before cooking to enhance the flavor.
- **Adjust Sweetness**: If you prefer a sweeter glaze, you can add a bit more honey. If you want more tang, increase the balsamic vinegar.
- **Side Suggestions**: This dish pairs well with roasted vegetables, mashed potatoes, or a simple salad.

Enjoy your pomegranate glazed pork chops! They're a flavorful and visually stunning dish that's perfect for a special occasion or a weeknight dinner.

Roasted Cauliflower with Parmesan

Ingredients

- **1 large head of cauliflower**, cut into florets
- **3 tbsp olive oil**
- **1/2 cup grated Parmesan cheese**
- **2 cloves garlic**, minced
- **1/2 tsp dried oregano** (or thyme)
- **Salt and black pepper**, to taste
- **1/4 cup chopped fresh parsley** (optional, for garnish)
- **Lemon wedges** (optional, for serving)

Instructions

1. **Preheat Oven**: Preheat your oven to 425°F (220°C).
2. **Prepare Cauliflower**:
   - Wash and cut the cauliflower into bite-sized florets.
   - Pat the florets dry with a paper towel to ensure they roast well.
3. **Season Cauliflower**:
   - In a large bowl, toss the cauliflower florets with olive oil, minced garlic, dried oregano (or thyme), salt, and black pepper until well coated.
4. **Roast Cauliflower**:
   - Spread the cauliflower in a single layer on a baking sheet. For best results, use parchment paper to prevent sticking and make cleanup easier.
   - Roast in the preheated oven for 20-25 minutes, or until the cauliflower is tender and golden brown, with crispy edges. Toss halfway through cooking to ensure even roasting.
5. **Add Parmesan**:
   - Remove the cauliflower from the oven and sprinkle the grated Parmesan cheese evenly over the top.
   - Return to the oven and roast for an additional 5 minutes, or until the cheese is melted and golden.
6. **Serve**:
   - Transfer the roasted cauliflower to a serving dish.
   - Garnish with chopped fresh parsley if desired.
   - Serve with lemon wedges on the side for a fresh, tangy touch.

Tips

- **For Extra Flavor**: You can add a pinch of red pepper flakes for a bit of heat or a sprinkle of smoked paprika for a smoky flavor.
- **Crispier Cauliflower**: For even crispier cauliflower, try roasting at a higher temperature (450°F or 230°C) and make sure not to overcrowd the baking sheet.
- **Make Ahead**: You can prep the cauliflower ahead of time and toss it with oil and seasonings, then refrigerate until you're ready to roast it.

This roasted cauliflower with Parmesan is a perfect side dish for any meal and is sure to be a hit with its delicious, cheesy flavor and crispy texture. Enjoy!

Buttery Garlic Mashed Potatoes

Ingredients

- **2 lbs (900g) russet or Yukon Gold potatoes**, peeled and cut into chunks
- **4 cloves garlic**, peeled
- **1/2 cup unsalted butter** (1 stick), plus more for serving
- **1/2 cup whole milk** (or heavy cream for extra richness)
- **Salt and black pepper**, to taste
- **2 tbsp chopped fresh chives** or **parsley** (optional, for garnish)

Instructions

1. **Prepare Potatoes and Garlic**:
   - Place the peeled and chunked potatoes and garlic cloves in a large pot.
   - Cover with cold water and add a generous pinch of salt.
2. **Cook Potatoes and Garlic**:
   - Bring the pot to a boil over high heat.
   - Reduce the heat to medium and simmer for about 15-20 minutes, or until the potatoes are fork-tender and the garlic cloves are soft.
3. **Drain and Dry**:
   - Drain the potatoes and garlic in a colander.
   - Return them to the pot and place over low heat for 1-2 minutes, stirring occasionally, to allow excess moisture to evaporate. This step helps make the potatoes creamier.
4. **Mash Potatoes**:
   - Use a potato masher or a ricer to mash the potatoes and garlic until smooth and free of lumps.
5. **Add Butter and Milk**:
   - In a small saucepan, heat the butter and milk until the butter is melted and the mixture is warm.
   - Pour the butter and milk mixture into the mashed potatoes and stir until well combined and creamy.
6. **Season**:
   - Season with salt and black pepper to taste.
   - Adjust the consistency by adding more milk if needed, or more butter for extra richness.
7. **Serve**:
   - Transfer the mashed potatoes to a serving dish.
   - Garnish with extra pats of butter and chopped fresh chives or parsley if desired.

Tips

- **For Creamier Potatoes**: Use heavy cream instead of milk for a richer, creamier texture.
- **For Extra Flavor**: Add a pinch of garlic powder or roasted garlic for even more garlic flavor.

- **Make Ahead**: You can prepare mashed potatoes a day in advance. Reheat them gently on the stovetop or in the oven, adding a bit more milk if needed to restore the creamy texture.

These buttery garlic mashed potatoes are perfect as a side dish for almost any meal, from weeknight dinners to holiday feasts. Enjoy!

Prosciutto Wrapped Asparagus

Ingredients

- **1 bunch asparagus** (about 12-15 spears)
- **6-8 slices of prosciutto** (or enough to wrap each asparagus spear)
- **2 tbsp olive oil**
- **1 tbsp balsamic vinegar** (optional, for a touch of acidity)
- **Salt and black pepper**, to taste
- **1 tbsp grated Parmesan cheese** (optional, for garnish)
- **Lemon wedges** (optional, for serving)

Instructions

1. **Preheat Oven**: Preheat your oven to 400°F (200°C).
2. **Prepare Asparagus**:
   - Trim the woody ends off the asparagus and discard. You can snap them off by gently bending the asparagus near the base, where it naturally breaks.
   - If the asparagus spears are very thick, you might want to peel the lower part of the stalks to ensure even cooking.
3. **Wrap Asparagus**:
   - Lay a slice of prosciutto on a cutting board. Place one asparagus spear at the end of the prosciutto slice.
   - Wrap the prosciutto around the asparagus spear, starting at one end and working your way to the other end. The prosciutto should overlap slightly as you wrap.
   - Repeat with the remaining asparagus and prosciutto.
4. **Prepare for Baking**:
   - Arrange the wrapped asparagus spears in a single layer on a baking sheet. For easier cleanup, you can line the baking sheet with parchment paper.
   - Drizzle the wrapped asparagus with olive oil and season lightly with salt and black pepper. Be careful with the salt as prosciutto is already salty.
5. **Bake**:
   - Bake in the preheated oven for 12-15 minutes, or until the asparagus is tender and the prosciutto is crispy. The exact time will depend on the thickness of the asparagus.
6. **Optional Balsamic Glaze**:
   - If using balsamic vinegar, you can drizzle a little over the asparagus after baking for a touch of acidity and extra flavor.
7. **Garnish and Serve**:
   - Transfer the prosciutto-wrapped asparagus to a serving platter.
   - Garnish with grated Parmesan cheese if desired and serve with lemon wedges for a fresh touch.

Tips

- **For Even Cooking**: Make sure the asparagus spears are of similar thickness for even cooking.
- **Serving Suggestions**: This dish works great as an appetizer, a side dish, or even a light main course. It pairs well with a crisp white wine or a sparkling water with a lemon slice.
- **Make Ahead**: You can prepare the wrapped asparagus ahead of time and refrigerate them until ready to bake. Just add a couple of extra minutes to the baking time if cooking straight from the fridge.

Prosciutto-wrapped asparagus is a flavorful and sophisticated dish that's sure to impress your guests. Enjoy!

Sweet Potato and Black Bean Enchiladas

Ingredients:

For the Filling:

- 2 medium sweet potatoes, peeled and cubed
- 1 tablespoon olive oil
- 1 teaspoon ground cumin
- 1 teaspoon smoked paprika
- 1/2 teaspoon chili powder
- 1/2 teaspoon garlic powder
- Salt and pepper, to taste
- 1 can (15 oz) black beans, drained and rinsed
- 1 cup corn kernels (fresh, frozen, or canned)
- 1 cup chopped red bell pepper
- 1/2 cup chopped red onion
- 1/4 cup chopped fresh cilantro (optional)

For the Enchilada Sauce:

- 1 tablespoon olive oil
- 1/4 cup chili powder
- 2 tablespoons all-purpose flour
- 1 can (15 oz) tomato sauce
- 1 cup vegetable broth
- 1/2 teaspoon ground cumin
- 1/2 teaspoon garlic powder
- Salt and pepper, to taste

For Assembly:

- 8-10 corn or flour tortillas
- 1 1/2 cups shredded cheese (cheddar, Monterey Jack, or a Mexican blend)
- Fresh cilantro, chopped (for garnish)
- Lime wedges (for serving)

Instructions:

1. Prepare the Sweet Potato Filling:

1. Preheat your oven to 400°F (200°C).
2. Toss the cubed sweet potatoes with olive oil, cumin, smoked paprika, chili powder, garlic powder, salt, and pepper.

3. Spread the sweet potatoes on a baking sheet and roast for 25-30 minutes, or until tender and lightly caramelized, stirring halfway through.
4. In a large bowl, combine the roasted sweet potatoes, black beans, corn, red bell pepper, red onion, and cilantro. Mix well.

2. Make the Enchilada Sauce:

1. In a medium saucepan, heat olive oil over medium heat.
2. Add the chili powder and flour, stirring constantly for about 1 minute until fragrant.
3. Gradually whisk in the tomato sauce and vegetable broth.
4. Stir in the cumin, garlic powder, salt, and pepper.
5. Bring the sauce to a simmer and cook for about 5-7 minutes, until slightly thickened. Adjust seasoning if needed.

3. Assemble the Enchiladas:

1. Preheat your oven to 375°F (190°C).
2. Lightly grease a 9x13-inch baking dish.
3. Spread a thin layer of enchilada sauce on the bottom of the dish.
4. Fill each tortilla with a generous amount of the sweet potato mixture. Roll up and place seam-side down in the baking dish.
5. Once all the tortillas are in the dish, pour the remaining enchilada sauce over the top.
6. Sprinkle shredded cheese evenly over the sauce.

4. Bake and Serve:

1. Cover the baking dish with foil and bake for 20 minutes.
2. Remove the foil and bake for an additional 10 minutes, or until the cheese is bubbly and golden brown.
3. Let the enchiladas cool slightly before serving.
4. Garnish with fresh cilantro and serve with lime wedges on the side.

Enjoy your sweet potato and black bean enchiladas! They're great on their own or served with a side of rice or a fresh salad.

Crab Cakes with Remoulade Sauce

Ingredients:

For the Crab Cakes:

- 1 pound (450g) fresh crab meat (lump or backfin)
- 1/2 cup mayonnaise
- 1 large egg
- 1 tablespoon Dijon mustard
- 1 tablespoon Old Bay seasoning
- 1 teaspoon Worcestershire sauce
- 1 teaspoon lemon juice
- 1/4 cup finely chopped fresh parsley
- 1/4 cup finely chopped green onions
- 1/4 cup finely chopped red bell pepper
- 1/4 cup breadcrumbs (plain or panko)
- Salt and black pepper, to taste
- 2 tablespoons olive oil or vegetable oil, for frying

For the Remoulade Sauce:

- 1/2 cup mayonnaise
- 2 tablespoons Dijon mustard
- 1 tablespoon lemon juice
- 1 tablespoon hot sauce (e.g., Tabasco)
- 1 tablespoon capers, chopped
- 1 tablespoon finely chopped fresh parsley
- 1 teaspoon paprika
- 1/2 teaspoon garlic powder
- Salt and black pepper, to taste

Instructions:

1. Prepare the Crab Cakes:

1. **Mix Ingredients:**
   - In a large bowl, gently combine the crab meat, mayonnaise, egg, Dijon mustard, Old Bay seasoning, Worcestershire sauce, lemon juice, parsley, green onions, red bell pepper, and breadcrumbs. Be careful not to break up the crab meat too much—just enough to mix everything together. Season with salt and pepper to taste.
2. **Form the Cakes:**

- Divide the mixture into 8-10 portions and shape each portion into a patty about 1/2 to 3/4 inch thick. Place the patties on a plate and refrigerate for at least 30 minutes to help them hold their shape.
3. **Cook the Cakes:**
    - Heat the olive oil or vegetable oil in a large skillet over medium heat.
    - Once the oil is hot, carefully add the crab cakes. Cook for about 4-5 minutes on each side, or until golden brown and crispy. Be gentle when flipping to avoid breaking the cakes.
4. **Drain and Serve:**
    - Transfer the cooked crab cakes to a plate lined with paper towels to drain any excess oil.

2. Make the Remoulade Sauce:

1. **Combine Ingredients:**
    - In a small bowl, mix together the mayonnaise, Dijon mustard, lemon juice, hot sauce, capers, parsley, paprika, and garlic powder. Season with salt and pepper to taste.
2. **Chill:**
    - Refrigerate the remoulade sauce until ready to use. It can be made a day in advance to allow the flavors to meld.

3. Serve:

- Serve the crab cakes warm with a generous dollop of remoulade sauce on the side. They pair well with a fresh salad, coleslaw, or a simple side of roasted vegetables.

Enjoy your homemade crab cakes with remoulade sauce! They're perfect for a special dinner or a delightful appetizer.

Chicken Alfredo Pasta

Ingredients:

For the Chicken:

- 2 tablespoons olive oil
- 2 large boneless, skinless chicken breasts (about 1 pound or 450g)
- Salt and black pepper, to taste
- 1/2 teaspoon garlic powder
- 1/2 teaspoon onion powder
- 1/2 teaspoon dried Italian herbs (optional)

For the Alfredo Sauce:

- 4 tablespoons unsalted butter
- 2 cloves garlic, minced
- 1 cup heavy cream
- 1 cup grated Parmesan cheese
- 1/4 teaspoon nutmeg (optional)
- Salt and black pepper, to taste

For the Pasta:

- 12 oz (340g) fettuccine or your favorite pasta
- 2 tablespoons chopped fresh parsley (for garnish)

Instructions:

1. Cook the Chicken:

1. **Season the Chicken:**
   - Season the chicken breasts with salt, pepper, garlic powder, onion powder, and Italian herbs (if using).
2. **Cook the Chicken:**
   - Heat olive oil in a large skillet over medium heat.
   - Add the chicken breasts and cook for about 6-7 minutes on each side, or until fully cooked and golden brown. The internal temperature should reach 165°F (75°C). Remove from the skillet and let rest for a few minutes before slicing.

2. Prepare the Pasta:

1. **Cook the Pasta:**
   - While the chicken is cooking, bring a large pot of salted water to a boil.
   - Add the fettuccine and cook according to the package instructions until al dente.
   - Drain the pasta and set aside.

3. Make the Alfredo Sauce:

1. **Prepare the Sauce:**
   - In the same skillet used for the chicken (you can wipe it out if needed), melt the butter over medium heat.
   - Add the minced garlic and sauté for about 1 minute, until fragrant.
   - Pour in the heavy cream and bring to a simmer. Reduce the heat and let it simmer gently for about 2-3 minutes.
2. **Add Cheese:**
   - Gradually whisk in the grated Parmesan cheese until the sauce is smooth and creamy.
   - Season with nutmeg (if using), salt, and black pepper to taste.

4. Combine and Serve:

1. **Mix Pasta and Sauce:**
   - Add the cooked pasta to the Alfredo sauce, tossing to coat the pasta evenly.
   - Slice the cooked chicken into strips and arrange on top of the pasta or mix it in.
2. **Garnish and Serve:**
   - Garnish with chopped fresh parsley for a touch of color and freshness.
   - Serve immediately.

Tips:

- For extra flavor, you can add a pinch of red pepper flakes to the sauce for some heat or sauté mushrooms and spinach to mix in with the pasta.
- Use freshly grated Parmesan cheese for the best texture and flavor. Pre-grated cheese may not melt as well and can result in a grainy sauce.

Enjoy your creamy and delicious Chicken Alfredo Pasta! It's perfect for a satisfying dinner or a special occasion.

Mediterranean Quinoa Salad

Ingredients:

For the Salad:

- 1 cup quinoa
- 2 cups water or vegetable broth
- 1 cup cherry or grape tomatoes, halved
- 1 cucumber, diced
- 1/2 red onion, finely chopped
- 1/2 cup Kalamata olives, pitted and sliced
- 1/2 cup crumbled feta cheese
- 1/4 cup fresh parsley, chopped
- 1/4 cup fresh mint, chopped (optional)
- 1/4 cup red or yellow bell pepper, diced (optional)

For the Dressing:

- 1/4 cup extra-virgin olive oil
- 2 tablespoons lemon juice
- 1 tablespoon red wine vinegar
- 1 teaspoon Dijon mustard
- 1 clove garlic, minced
- 1/2 teaspoon dried oregano
- Salt and black pepper, to taste

Instructions:

1. Cook the Quinoa:

1. **Rinse the Quinoa:**
   - Rinse the quinoa under cold water in a fine-mesh sieve to remove any bitterness.
2. **Cook the Quinoa:**
   - In a medium saucepan, combine the quinoa and water or vegetable broth.
   - Bring to a boil over high heat, then reduce to a simmer.
   - Cover and cook for about 15 minutes, or until the quinoa is tender and the liquid is absorbed.
   - Remove from heat and let it sit, covered, for 5 minutes. Fluff with a fork and let it cool to room temperature.

2. Prepare the Vegetables:

1. **Chop Vegetables:**
   - While the quinoa is cooling, prepare the cherry tomatoes, cucumber, red onion, olives, and any optional ingredients like bell pepper.

3. Make the Dressing:

1. **Combine Ingredients:**
   - In a small bowl or jar, whisk together the olive oil, lemon juice, red wine vinegar, Dijon mustard, minced garlic, dried oregano, salt, and black pepper.

4. Assemble the Salad:

1. **Mix Ingredients:**
   - In a large bowl, combine the cooked quinoa, cherry tomatoes, cucumber, red onion, olives, feta cheese, parsley, and mint (if using).
2. **Add Dressing:**
   - Pour the dressing over the salad and toss gently to combine.

5. Serve:

1. **Chill (Optional):**
   - You can serve the salad immediately or chill it in the refrigerator for at least 30 minutes to allow the flavors to meld.
2. **Garnish:**
   - Garnish with additional chopped parsley or mint if desired before serving.

Tips:

- This salad can be made ahead of time and stored in the refrigerator for up to 3 days.
- For added protein, you can mix in some cooked chickpeas or grilled chicken.
- Adjust the seasoning according to your taste. Some might prefer a bit more lemon juice or a pinch of crushed red pepper flakes for extra zing.

Enjoy your Mediterranean Quinoa Salad as a healthy lunch, side dish, or a light dinner!

Beef Bourguignon

Ingredients:

For the Beef Bourguignon:

- 3 pounds (1.4 kg) beef chuck, cut into 1.5-inch cubes
- Salt and black pepper, to taste
- 2-3 tablespoons vegetable oil
- 4 slices bacon, chopped
- 1 large onion, chopped
- 2 carrots, peeled and sliced
- 2 cloves garlic, minced
- 2 tablespoons tomato paste
- 1/4 cup all-purpose flour
- 3 cups red wine (preferably Burgundy or Pinot Noir)
- 2 cups beef broth
- 2 bay leaves
- 1 teaspoon dried thyme
- 1 cup pearl onions, peeled (frozen or fresh)
- 1 cup mushrooms, quartered
- 2 tablespoons unsalted butter (for sautéing mushrooms)

For Garnish (Optional):

- Fresh parsley, chopped

Instructions:

1. Prepare the Beef:

1. **Season the Beef:**
   - Pat the beef cubes dry with paper towels and season with salt and black pepper.
2. **Brown the Beef:**
   - Heat vegetable oil in a large Dutch oven or heavy-bottomed pot over medium-high heat.
   - In batches, brown the beef on all sides, ensuring not to overcrowd the pot. Remove the beef and set aside.

2. Cook the Bacon and Vegetables:

1. **Cook Bacon:**
   - In the same pot, add the chopped bacon and cook until crispy. Remove the bacon with a slotted spoon and set aside.
2. **Sauté Vegetables:**

- Add the chopped onion and sliced carrots to the pot. Cook until softened, about 5-7 minutes.
- Stir in the minced garlic and tomato paste, cooking for an additional 1-2 minutes.

3. Combine and Simmer:

1. **Add Flour:**
   - Sprinkle the flour over the vegetables and stir to combine. Cook for about 2 minutes to get rid of the raw flour taste.
2. **Deglaze the Pot:**
   - Pour in the red wine, scraping the bottom of the pot to loosen any browned bits.
3. **Add Broth and Herbs:**
   - Return the browned beef and bacon to the pot.
   - Add the beef broth, bay leaves, and dried thyme. Stir to combine.
4. **Simmer:**
   - Bring the mixture to a boil, then reduce the heat to low.
   - Cover and simmer for 2.5 to 3 hours, or until the beef is tender and the sauce is thickened.

4. Prepare the Pearl Onions and Mushrooms:

1. **Sauté Mushrooms:**
   - While the beef is simmering, heat the butter in a skillet over medium heat.
   - Add the quartered mushrooms and cook until browned and tender, about 8-10 minutes. Set aside.
2. **Cook Pearl Onions:**
   - If using fresh pearl onions, blanch them in boiling water for 1-2 minutes, then peel.
   - Sauté the pearl onions in a little butter or oil until browned and tender, about 5-7 minutes. Set aside.

5. Final Touches:

1. **Add Mushrooms and Onions:**
   - About 30 minutes before the beef is done, add the sautéed mushrooms and pearl onions to the pot. Stir to combine.
2. **Adjust Seasoning:**
   - Taste and adjust seasoning with additional salt and pepper if needed.

6. Serve:

1. **Garnish and Serve:**
   - Remove the bay leaves.
   - Garnish with chopped fresh parsley if desired.
   - Serve the Beef Bourguignon over mashed potatoes, noodles, or with crusty bread for a complete meal.

Tips:

- For an even richer flavor, you can marinate the beef in red wine and herbs overnight before cooking.
- If you prefer a thicker sauce, you can mix a tablespoon of cornstarch with a little water and stir it into the sauce to thicken.

Enjoy your Beef Bourguignon! It's a comforting, savory dish perfect for special occasions or a cozy meal at home.

Honey Mustard Glazed Carrots

Ingredients:

- 1 pound (450g) carrots, peeled and cut into bite-sized pieces (or baby carrots)
- 2 tablespoons olive oil
- Salt and black pepper, to taste

For the Glaze:

- 3 tablespoons honey
- 2 tablespoons Dijon mustard
- 1 tablespoon whole grain mustard (optional, for extra texture)
- 1 tablespoon butter
- 1 tablespoon apple cider vinegar or white wine vinegar
- 1 clove garlic, minced (optional)
- 1 teaspoon dried thyme or rosemary (optional)
- Fresh parsley, chopped (for garnish, optional)

Instructions:

1. Prepare the Carrots:

1. **Preheat Oven:**
   - Preheat your oven to 400°F (200°C).
2. **Season Carrots:**
   - In a large bowl, toss the carrot pieces with olive oil, salt, and black pepper.
3. **Roast Carrots:**
   - Spread the carrots in a single layer on a baking sheet.
   - Roast in the preheated oven for 25-30 minutes, or until the carrots are tender and slightly caramelized, stirring once halfway through.

2. Make the Honey Mustard Glaze:

1. **Combine Glaze Ingredients:**
   - In a small saucepan, melt the butter over medium heat.
   - Add the honey, Dijon mustard, whole grain mustard (if using), vinegar, and minced garlic (if using).
   - Stir until the mixture is smooth and heated through. If you're using dried thyme or rosemary, add it at this stage. Cook for 1-2 minutes until fragrant.
2. **Adjust Flavor:**
   - Taste the glaze and adjust the seasoning if needed, adding more honey for sweetness, mustard for tanginess, or vinegar for acidity.

3. Combine Carrots and Glaze:

1. **Toss Carrots:**
   - Once the carrots are roasted, remove them from the oven.
   - Transfer the carrots to a large bowl or back to the baking sheet.
2. **Add Glaze:**
   - Pour the honey mustard glaze over the roasted carrots and toss to coat evenly.
3. **Optional Final Touch:**
   - For extra flavor, you can return the glazed carrots to the oven for an additional 5 minutes to allow the glaze to caramelize slightly.

4. Garnish and Serve:

1. **Garnish:**
   - Garnish with chopped fresh parsley if desired.
2. **Serve:**
   - Serve warm as a delicious side dish with your favorite main courses.

Tips:

- For a quicker preparation, you can use pre-cut baby carrots.
- You can also make the glaze ahead of time and store it in the refrigerator. Just reheat it before using.
- Feel free to experiment with different herbs or spices to match your meal's flavor profile.

Enjoy your Honey Mustard Glazed Carrots! They're a fantastic way to elevate your vegetable side dishes with a sweet and tangy twist.

Lobster Newberg

Ingredients:

- **For the Lobster:**
    - 1 1/2 to 2 pounds (680-900g) lobster (about 2 whole lobsters or 4-6 tails)
    - Salt
    - Water (for boiling)
- **For the Newberg Sauce:**
    - 2 tablespoons unsalted butter
    - 1 small onion, finely chopped
    - 1 cup heavy cream
    - 1/2 cup chicken or seafood broth
    - 1/4 cup dry white wine or sherry
    - 4 large egg yolks
    - 1 tablespoon all-purpose flour
    - 1/4 teaspoon paprika
    - 1/4 teaspoon cayenne pepper (optional)
    - Salt and black pepper, to taste
    - 2 tablespoons fresh lemon juice
    - 2 tablespoons chopped fresh parsley (optional)
    - 1 tablespoon fresh chives, chopped (optional)
- **For Serving:**
    - 4 slices of buttered toast or puff pastry shells

Instructions:

1. Prepare the Lobster:

1. **Boil Lobster:**
    - Bring a large pot of salted water to a boil.
    - Add the lobsters and cook for about 8-10 minutes for whole lobsters, or 5-7 minutes for lobster tails, until the shells are bright red and the lobster meat is opaque.
    - Remove the lobsters from the pot and let them cool.
2. **Extract Meat:**
    - Once cool enough to handle, remove the lobster meat from the shells. Discard the shells and any sac (the small, soft stomach sac) in the lobster head.
    - Cut the lobster meat into bite-sized pieces.

2. Make the Newberg Sauce:

1. **Sauté Onions:**
    - In a medium saucepan, melt the butter over medium heat.
    - Add the finely chopped onion and cook until softened, about 2-3 minutes.

2. **Prepare Sauce:**
   - Stir in the flour and cook for about 1 minute to make a roux.
   - Gradually whisk in the heavy cream, chicken or seafood broth, and white wine or sherry.
   - Bring the mixture to a simmer, stirring constantly, until it begins to thicken (about 3-5 minutes).
3. **Add Egg Yolks:**
   - In a small bowl, lightly beat the egg yolks.
   - Temper the egg yolks by adding a few spoonfuls of the hot sauce to the yolks, then slowly whisk the yolk mixture back into the saucepan.
   - Continue to cook on low heat, stirring constantly, until the sauce is thickened and smooth (do not let it boil).
4. **Season:**
   - Stir in the paprika, cayenne pepper (if using), salt, and black pepper.
   - Add the fresh lemon juice and adjust seasoning to taste.

3. Combine and Serve:

1. **Add Lobster Meat:**
   - Gently fold the lobster meat into the sauce, cooking for just a few minutes until the lobster is heated through.
2. **Prepare Toast or Puff Pastry:**
   - If using toast, butter and toast the bread slices until golden brown.
   - If using puff pastry shells, bake according to package instructions or your recipe until golden and crisp.
3. **Serve:**
   - Spoon the lobster mixture over the toast or into the puff pastry shells.
   - Garnish with chopped fresh parsley and chives if desired.

Tips:

- For a richer flavor, you can add a splash of brandy or cognac to the sauce.
- Make sure not to overcook the lobster or the sauce, as this can make the lobster tough and the sauce curdle.

Enjoy your Lobster Newberg! It's a decadent and flavorful dish perfect for special occasions or a luxurious treat.

Baked Ziti with Sausage

Ingredients:

- **For the Pasta and Sauce:**
    - 1 pound (450g) ziti or penne pasta
    - 1 pound (450g) Italian sausage (mild or spicy, as preferred)
    - 1 tablespoon olive oil
    - 1 medium onion, finely chopped
    - 2 cloves garlic, minced
    - 1 can (28 oz) crushed tomatoes
    - 1 can (15 oz) tomato sauce
    - 2 tablespoons tomato paste
    - 1 teaspoon dried oregano
    - 1 teaspoon dried basil
    - 1/2 teaspoon red pepper flakes (optional, for heat)
    - Salt and black pepper, to taste
- **For the Cheese Mixture:**
    - 2 cups ricotta cheese
    - 1 cup grated Parmesan cheese
    - 1 large egg
    - 1 cup shredded mozzarella cheese (for mixing)
- **For the Topping:**
    - 1 1/2 cups shredded mozzarella cheese
    - Fresh basil or parsley, chopped (for garnish, optional)

Instructions:

1. Prepare the Pasta:

1. **Cook the Pasta:**
    - Preheat your oven to 375°F (190°C).
    - Bring a large pot of salted water to a boil.
    - Cook the ziti according to package instructions until al dente. Drain and set aside.

2. Make the Sauce:

1. **Cook the Sausage:**
    - In a large skillet or Dutch oven, heat the olive oil over medium heat.
    - Remove the sausage from its casing and crumble it into the skillet.
    - Cook until browned and fully cooked, breaking it up with a spoon as it cooks. Remove the sausage from the skillet and set aside.
2. **Sauté Onions and Garlic:**
    - In the same skillet, add the chopped onion and cook until softened, about 5 minutes.

- Add the minced garlic and cook for another 1 minute until fragrant.
3. **Combine Sauce Ingredients:**
    - Stir in the crushed tomatoes, tomato sauce, tomato paste, dried oregano, dried basil, and red pepper flakes (if using).
    - Return the cooked sausage to the skillet.
    - Simmer the sauce for 15-20 minutes, allowing the flavors to meld. Season with salt and black pepper to taste.

3. Prepare the Cheese Mixture:

1. **Mix Cheese Ingredients:**
    - In a medium bowl, combine the ricotta cheese, grated Parmesan cheese, and egg.
    - Stir in 1 cup of shredded mozzarella cheese.

4. Assemble the Baked Ziti:

1. **Combine Pasta and Sauce:**
    - In a large bowl, mix the cooked ziti with the sausage sauce, ensuring the pasta is well coated.
2. **Layer Ingredients:**
    - In a greased 9x13-inch baking dish, spread a thin layer of the pasta sauce mixture.
    - Spoon half of the cheese mixture over the pasta.
    - Add the remaining pasta sauce mixture and spread evenly.
3. **Top with Cheese:**
    - Sprinkle the remaining 1 1/2 cups of shredded mozzarella cheese over the top.

5. Bake:

1. **Bake the Dish:**
    - Cover the baking dish with aluminum foil and bake in the preheated oven for 20 minutes.
    - Remove the foil and bake for an additional 15-20 minutes, or until the top is golden and bubbly.
2. **Cool and Serve:**
    - Let the baked ziti cool for about 10 minutes before serving.
    - Garnish with chopped fresh basil or parsley if desired.

Tips:

- **Make Ahead:** You can assemble the baked ziti a day in advance and refrigerate it before baking. Just add a few extra minutes to the baking time.
- **Freezing:** Baked ziti can be frozen before baking. Wrap it tightly with foil and freeze for up to 3 months. Thaw overnight in the refrigerator before baking.

Enjoy your hearty and satisfying Baked Ziti with Sausage! It's perfect for feeding a crowd and pairs wonderfully with a simple green salad and garlic bread.

Parmesan Crusted Salmon

Ingredients:

- 4 salmon fillets (about 6 ounces each)
- Salt and black pepper, to taste
- 1 tablespoon olive oil
- 1/2 cup grated Parmesan cheese
- 1/2 cup panko breadcrumbs
- 2 tablespoons chopped fresh parsley (or 1 tablespoon dried parsley)
- 1 teaspoon garlic powder
- 1 teaspoon dried thyme (or Italian seasoning)
- 1 tablespoon Dijon mustard (optional, for extra flavor)

Instructions:

1. Prepare the Salmon:

1. **Preheat Oven:**
    - Preheat your oven to 400°F (200°C).
2. **Season the Salmon:**
    - Pat the salmon fillets dry with paper towels.
    - Season both sides of the fillets with salt and black pepper.

2. Prepare the Parmesan Crust:

1. **Combine Crust Ingredients:**
    - In a small bowl, mix together the grated Parmesan cheese, panko breadcrumbs, chopped parsley, garlic powder, and dried thyme (or Italian seasoning).
2. **Add Dijon Mustard (Optional):**
    - For an extra layer of flavor, you can spread a thin layer of Dijon mustard on the top of each salmon fillet before adding the crust mixture.

3. Assemble the Dish:

1. **Apply the Crust:**
    - Place the salmon fillets skin-side down on a baking sheet lined with parchment paper or lightly greased.
    - Press the Parmesan mixture onto the top of each fillet, ensuring an even layer.
2. **Drizzle with Olive Oil:**
    - Drizzle a little olive oil over the top of the Parmesan crust to help it brown and crisp up.

4. Bake the Salmon:

1. **Bake:**
    - Bake in the preheated oven for about 12-15 minutes, or until the salmon is cooked through and flakes easily with a fork. The crust should be golden brown and crispy.
2. **Check Doneness:**

- If you have a food thermometer, the internal temperature of the salmon should reach 145°F (63°C).

5. Serve:

1. **Garnish:**
   - Garnish with additional fresh parsley if desired.
2. **Serve:**
   - Serve the Parmesan Crusted Salmon with your favorite sides, such as roasted vegetables, a fresh salad, or rice.

Tips:

- **Customize the Crust:** Feel free to add other seasonings or herbs to the crust mixture to suit your taste.
- **Ensure Crispiness:** For an extra crispy crust, you can broil the salmon for the last 2-3 minutes of baking, but watch it closely to avoid burning.
- **Make Ahead:** You can prepare the Parmesan mixture and season the salmon a few hours in advance. Store in the refrigerator until ready to bake.

Enjoy your Parmesan Crusted Salmon! It's a flavorful, elegant dish that's perfect for a quick weeknight dinner or a special occasion.

Stuffed Acorn Squash

Ingredients:

- **For the Acorn Squash:**
  - 2 medium acorn squashes
  - 2 tablespoons olive oil
  - Salt and black pepper, to taste
- **For the Stuffing:**
  - 1 cup cooked quinoa, rice, or couscous
  - 1/2 cup finely chopped onion
  - 2 cloves garlic, minced
  - 1 cup diced bell pepper (any color)
  - 1 cup chopped fresh spinach or kale (optional)
  - 1/2 cup dried cranberries or raisins
  - 1/2 cup chopped nuts (e.g., walnuts, pecans, or almonds)
  - 1/2 cup crumbled feta cheese or shredded cheese of choice
  - 1 teaspoon dried thyme
  - 1/2 teaspoon ground cumin (optional)
  - 1/4 teaspoon ground cinnamon (optional)
  - Salt and black pepper, to taste
- **For Garnish (Optional):**
  - Fresh parsley or thyme

Instructions:

1. Prepare the Acorn Squash:

1. **Preheat Oven:**
   - Preheat your oven to 400°F (200°C).
2. **Prepare Squash:**
   - Cut each acorn squash in half lengthwise and scoop out the seeds.
   - Brush the cut sides with olive oil and season with salt and black pepper.
3. **Roast Squash:**
   - Place the squash halves cut-side down on a baking sheet lined with parchment paper or aluminum foil.
   - Roast in the preheated oven for 25-30 minutes, or until the squash is tender when pierced with a fork.

2. Prepare the Stuffing:

1. **Cook the Vegetables:**
   - While the squash is roasting, heat a tablespoon of olive oil in a skillet over medium heat.
   - Add the chopped onion and cook until softened, about 5 minutes.
   - Stir in the minced garlic and cook for another minute.
2. **Add Bell Pepper and Greens:**
   - Add the diced bell pepper and cook until tender, about 5 minutes.
   - If using spinach or kale, add it now and cook until wilted.

3. **Mix in Remaining Ingredients:**
   - In a large bowl, combine the cooked quinoa (or rice or couscous), sautéed vegetables, dried cranberries or raisins, chopped nuts, and crumbled feta cheese.
   - Stir in the dried thyme, ground cumin (if using), ground cinnamon (if using), salt, and black pepper. Mix until well combined.

3. Stuff the Squash:

1. **Fill Squash Halves:**
   - Remove the squash from the oven and carefully flip the halves cut-side up.
   - Spoon the stuffing mixture into each squash half, packing it in gently.
2. **Return to Oven:**
   - Return the stuffed squash to the oven and bake for an additional 10-15 minutes, or until the stuffing is heated through and the top is slightly golden.

4. Garnish and Serve:

1. **Garnish:**
   - Garnish with fresh parsley or thyme if desired.
2. **Serve:**
   - Serve the stuffed acorn squash warm as a main course or side dish.

Tips:

- **Make Ahead:** The stuffing can be prepared a day in advance and stored in the refrigerator. Stuff the squash and bake it on the day you plan to serve.
- **Substitute Ingredients:** Feel free to customize the stuffing with other vegetables, cheeses, or proteins according to your taste preferences.
- **For Extra Flavor:** You can add a drizzle of balsamic glaze or a sprinkle of toasted breadcrumbs on top of the stuffed squash before the final baking.

Enjoy your Stuffed Acorn Squash! It's a wonderfully versatile and satisfying dish that's perfect for fall and winter meals.

Sautéed Green Beans with Almonds

Ingredients:

- 1 pound (450g) fresh green beans, trimmed

- 2 tablespoons olive oil or unsalted butter
- 2 cloves garlic, minced
- 1/4 cup sliced almonds
- Salt and black pepper, to taste
- 1 tablespoon lemon juice (optional, for a touch of brightness)
- 1/2 teaspoon lemon zest (optional, for extra flavor)
- Fresh parsley, chopped (for garnish, optional)

Instructions:

1. Prepare the Green Beans:

1. **Trim Beans:**
   - Trim the ends of the green beans and rinse them under cold water.
2. **Blanch Beans (Optional but recommended for color and texture):**
   - Bring a large pot of salted water to a boil.
   - Add the green beans and cook for 2-3 minutes, or until bright green and just tender.
   - Immediately transfer the beans to a bowl of ice water to stop the cooking process.
   - Drain and pat dry.

2. Sauté the Green Beans:

1. **Heat Oil or Butter:**
   - In a large skillet, heat the olive oil or melt the butter over medium heat.
2. **Cook Garlic:**
   - Add the minced garlic to the skillet and cook for about 30 seconds, or until fragrant. Be careful not to burn the garlic.
3. **Add Green Beans:**
   - Add the green beans to the skillet. Cook, stirring occasionally, for about 5-7 minutes, or until they are heated through and start to get a bit of color.
4. **Add Almonds:**
   - Stir in the sliced almonds and cook for an additional 2-3 minutes, or until the almonds are lightly toasted and the beans are crisp-tender.

3. Season and Finish:

1. **Season:**
   - Season with salt and black pepper to taste.
   - If using, add the lemon juice and lemon zest for extra flavor and brightness.
2. **Garnish:**
   - Garnish with chopped fresh parsley if desired.

4. Serve:

1. **Serve:**
   - Serve the sautéed green beans warm as a side dish with your favorite main courses.

Tips:

- **Adjust Texture:** For extra crispness, avoid overcooking the green beans. They should be tender but still have a slight crunch.
- **Add Flavor Variations:** You can add other seasonings like crushed red pepper flakes for a bit of heat or a sprinkle of Parmesan cheese for added richness.
- **Make Ahead:** You can blanch the green beans a day in advance and store them in the refrigerator. Just sauté them with garlic and almonds when ready to serve.

Enjoy your Sautéed Green Beans with Almonds! It's a delicious and nutritious side dish that pairs well with a variety of main courses.

Bacon-Wrapped Dates

Ingredients:

- 20 large Medjool dates (pitted)
- 10 slices of bacon (cut in half)

- 1/4 cup almond or pecan halves (optional, for stuffing)
- 1 tablespoon honey (optional, for drizzling)
- Fresh thyme or rosemary (optional, for garnish)

Instructions:

1. Prepare the Dates:

1. **Preheat Oven:**
   - Preheat your oven to 375°F (190°C).
2. **Pit the Dates:**
   - If not already pitted, carefully slice open the dates and remove the pits.
3. **Stuff the Dates (Optional):**
   - If using, place an almond or pecan half inside each date for added texture and flavor.

2. Wrap with Bacon:

1. **Wrap Dates:**
   - Wrap each date with a half slice of bacon. Secure with a toothpick to hold the bacon in place.

3. Bake the Dates:

1. **Arrange on Baking Sheet:**
   - Place the wrapped dates on a baking sheet lined with parchment paper or a wire rack set over a baking sheet (for extra crispiness).
2. **Bake:**
   - Bake in the preheated oven for 15-20 minutes, or until the bacon is crispy and the dates are caramelized. Flip the dates halfway through baking for even crispiness.

4. Optional Finishing Touches:

1. **Drizzle with Honey (Optional):**
   - For a touch of extra sweetness, drizzle the dates with honey as soon as they come out of the oven.
2. **Garnish (Optional):**
   - Garnish with fresh thyme or rosemary if desired.

5. Serve:

1. **Serve Warm:**
   - Serve the bacon-wrapped dates warm or at room temperature. They can be enjoyed as an appetizer, snack, or party finger food.

Tips:

- **Cooking Time:** Adjust the cooking time based on the thickness of your bacon and how crispy you like it. Thin bacon may cook faster, so keep an eye on it.
- **Make Ahead:** You can prepare the dates and wrap them with bacon ahead of time. Store them in the refrigerator and bake them just before serving.
- **Variations:** Try adding a small amount of blue cheese or goat cheese inside the dates for a creamy, tangy twist.

Enjoy your Bacon-Wrapped Dates! They're a fantastic combination of sweet, savory, and crunchy, making them a crowd-pleaser at any event.

Grilled Vegetable Platter

Ingredients:

- **Vegetables:**
    - 2 bell peppers (red, yellow, or orange), cut into large chunks
    - 1 large zucchini, sliced into 1/2-inch thick rounds
    - 1 large yellow squash, sliced into 1/2-inch thick rounds

- 1 red onion, cut into wedges
- 8 oz (225g) cherry tomatoes (optional, for added color)
- 8 oz (225g) mushrooms (cremini or button), whole or halved if large
- 1 eggplant, sliced into 1/2-inch thick rounds
- 1 cup asparagus spears (woody ends trimmed)
- **For the Marinade:**
    - 1/4 cup olive oil
    - 2 tablespoons balsamic vinegar or red wine vinegar
    - 2 cloves garlic, minced
    - 1 tablespoon fresh rosemary or thyme (or 1 teaspoon dried)
    - 1 teaspoon dried oregano
    - 1 teaspoon paprika
    - Salt and black pepper, to taste
- **For Garnish (Optional):**
    - Fresh basil or parsley, chopped
    - Crumbled feta cheese or shaved Parmesan (optional)

Instructions:

1. Prepare the Vegetables:

1. **Wash and Cut:**
   - Wash and cut all vegetables as described above. Aim for uniform sizes to ensure even cooking.
2. **Prepare the Marinade:**
   - In a small bowl, whisk together the olive oil, balsamic vinegar, minced garlic, rosemary or thyme, dried oregano, paprika, salt, and black pepper.

2. Marinate the Vegetables:

1. **Marinate:**
   - Place the cut vegetables in a large bowl or resealable plastic bag.
   - Pour the marinade over the vegetables and toss to coat evenly.
   - Let them marinate for at least 15-30 minutes to absorb the flavors.

3. Preheat the Grill:

1. **Heat Grill:**
   - Preheat your grill to medium-high heat. If using a charcoal grill, ensure the coals are hot and have a consistent heat.
2. **Prepare Grill Grates:**
   - Lightly oil the grill grates or use a grill basket to prevent sticking.

4. Grill the Vegetables:

1. **Grill Vegetables:**
   - Place the vegetables directly on the grill grates or in a grill basket.
   - Grill the vegetables, turning occasionally, until they are tender and have nice grill marks. This usually takes about 8-12 minutes, depending on the type and thickness of the vegetables.
   - Cherry tomatoes can be grilled in a grill basket or on a skewer for easier handling.

5. Serve:

1. **Arrange on Platter:**
   - Transfer the grilled vegetables to a large serving platter.
2. **Garnish:**
   - Garnish with chopped fresh basil or parsley, and sprinkle with crumbled feta cheese or shaved Parmesan if desired.
3. **Serve:**
   - Serve warm or at room temperature.

Tips:

- **Uniform Sizes:** Cutting vegetables into similar sizes helps ensure they cook evenly.
- **Grill Basket:** Using a grill basket is particularly useful for smaller or more delicate vegetables like cherry tomatoes and mushrooms.
- **Make Ahead:** The vegetables can be marinated a day in advance. Grill them just before serving for the best texture and flavor.

Enjoy your Grilled Vegetable Platter! It's a vibrant, healthy dish that's sure to impress and satisfy your guests.

Classic Beef Chili

Ingredients:

- **For the Chili:**
  - 1 tablespoon olive oil
  - 1 large onion, chopped
  - 2 cloves garlic, minced

- 1 pound (450g) ground beef (85% lean or higher)
- 1 bell pepper, chopped (any color)
- 1 can (14.5 oz) diced tomatoes
- 1 can (15 oz) tomato sauce
- 1 can (15 oz) kidney beans, drained and rinsed
- 1 can (15 oz) black beans, drained and rinsed
- 1 cup beef broth or water
- 2 tablespoons chili powder
- 1 teaspoon ground cumin
- 1 teaspoon smoked paprika (optional, for a smoky flavor)
- 1/2 teaspoon dried oregano
- 1/2 teaspoon garlic powder
- 1/2 teaspoon onion powder
- Salt and black pepper, to taste

- **Optional Toppings:**
    - Shredded cheese
    - Sour cream
    - Sliced jalapeños
    - Chopped fresh cilantro
    - Sliced green onions
    - Tortilla chips or cornbread (for serving)

Instructions:

1. Cook the Beef and Vegetables:

1. **Heat Oil:**
    - In a large pot or Dutch oven, heat the olive oil over medium heat.
2. **Sauté Onion and Garlic:**
    - Add the chopped onion and cook until softened, about 5 minutes.
    - Add the minced garlic and cook for another 1 minute.
3. **Brown the Beef:**
    - Add the ground beef to the pot. Cook, breaking it up with a spoon, until browned and cooked through. Drain any excess fat if needed.
4. **Add Bell Pepper:**
    - Stir in the chopped bell pepper and cook for another 3-4 minutes until softened.

2. Add the Remaining Ingredients:

1. **Combine Ingredients:**
    - Stir in the diced tomatoes, tomato sauce, kidney beans, black beans, and beef broth (or water).
2. **Season:**
    - Add the chili powder, ground cumin, smoked paprika (if using), dried oregano, garlic powder, onion powder, salt, and black pepper.

3. Simmer the Chili:

1. **Bring to a Simmer:**
   - Bring the chili to a boil over medium-high heat.
2. **Reduce Heat and Simmer:**
   - Reduce the heat to low and let the chili simmer uncovered for about 30-45 minutes, stirring occasionally, until it thickens and the flavors meld together.

4. Adjust Seasoning and Serve:

1. **Taste and Adjust:**
   - Taste the chili and adjust the seasoning with more salt, pepper, or chili powder as needed.
2. **Serve:**
   - Ladle the chili into bowls and top with your favorite toppings such as shredded cheese, sour cream, sliced jalapeños, chopped cilantro, or green onions.
   - Serve with tortilla chips or cornbread if desired.

Tips:

- **Make Ahead:** Chili often tastes even better the next day as the flavors continue to develop. You can make it a day in advance and reheat it when ready to serve.
- **Freeze:** Chili freezes well. Let it cool completely before transferring it to an airtight container or freezer bag. It can be frozen for up to 3 months. Thaw in the refrigerator before reheating.
- **Adjust Heat:** If you like it spicier, add more chili powder, cayenne pepper, or diced jalapeños.

Enjoy your Classic Beef Chili! It's a warming, satisfying dish that's sure to be a hit at any meal.

Shrimp and Grits

Ingredients:

- **For the Grits:**
   - 1 cup stone-ground grits
   - 4 cups water or chicken broth
   - 1/2 cup milk or cream
   - 2 tablespoons unsalted butter

- 1 cup shredded sharp cheddar cheese (optional, for extra creaminess)
- Salt and black pepper, to taste
- **For the Shrimp:**
  - 1 pound (450g) large shrimp, peeled and deveined
  - 2 tablespoons olive oil
  - 4 slices bacon, chopped
  - 1 small onion, finely chopped
  - 2 cloves garlic, minced
  - 1/2 cup chicken broth
  - 1 tablespoon lemon juice
  - 1 teaspoon paprika
  - 1/2 teaspoon dried thyme
  - 1/2 teaspoon dried oregano
  - 1/4 teaspoon cayenne pepper (optional, for heat)
  - Salt and black pepper, to taste
  - 2 tablespoons chopped fresh parsley (for garnish)

Instructions:

1. Prepare the Grits:

1. **Cook Grits:**
   - In a large saucepan, bring the water or chicken broth to a boil.
   - Gradually whisk in the grits. Reduce the heat to low and cover. Cook the grits, stirring occasionally, for about 20-25 minutes, or until thickened and tender.
2. **Finish Grits:**
   - Stir in the milk or cream and butter. If using, mix in the shredded cheddar cheese until melted and smooth.
   - Season with salt and black pepper to taste. Keep warm.

2. Prepare the Shrimp:

1. **Cook Bacon:**
   - In a large skillet, cook the chopped bacon over medium heat until crispy. Remove the bacon with a slotted spoon and set aside, leaving the drippings in the skillet.
2. **Sauté Onions and Garlic:**
   - Add the finely chopped onion to the skillet and cook in the bacon drippings until softened, about 3-4 minutes.
   - Add the minced garlic and cook for another 1 minute until fragrant.
3. **Cook Shrimp:**
   - Increase the heat to medium-high and add the shrimp to the skillet. Cook for about 2-3 minutes on each side, or until the shrimp are pink and opaque.
4. **Add Flavorings:**
   - Stir in the chicken broth, lemon juice, paprika, dried thyme, dried oregano, cayenne pepper (if using), salt, and black pepper.

            - Simmer for 2-3 minutes until the sauce has slightly reduced.
    5. **Add Bacon:**
        - Return the cooked bacon to the skillet and stir to combine.

3. Serve:

1. **Plate the Dish:**
    - Spoon the creamy grits onto plates or bowls.
    - Top with the shrimp mixture and drizzle with the sauce from the skillet.
2. **Garnish:**
    - Garnish with chopped fresh parsley.

Tips:

- **For Extra Creaminess:** Use a mix of water and milk or cream to cook the grits for a richer texture. Adding cheese is optional but recommended for a more indulgent version.
- **Spice Level:** Adjust the amount of cayenne pepper according to your preference for heat.
- **Make Ahead:** You can prepare the grits ahead of time and reheat them gently. The shrimp should be cooked just before serving for the best texture.

Enjoy your Shrimp and Grits! It's a flavorful and satisfying dish that brings together classic Southern ingredients in a delightful way.

Thai Green Curry with Chicken

Ingredients:

- **For the Curry:**
    - 1 tablespoon vegetable oil
    - 2-3 tablespoons Thai green curry paste (adjust based on your spice preference)
    - 1 pound (450g) boneless, skinless chicken thighs or breasts, cut into bite-sized pieces

- 1 can (13.5 oz) coconut milk
- 1 cup chicken broth
- 2 tablespoons fish sauce
- 1 tablespoon brown sugar or palm sugar
- 1-2 Thai bird chilies or red chili (optional, for extra heat)
- 1-2 kaffir lime leaves (optional, for extra flavor)
- 1 tablespoon chopped fresh basil (Thai basil if available) or cilantro
- **For the Vegetables:**
  - 1 cup sliced bell peppers (red, green, or yellow)
  - 1 cup sliced carrots
  - 1 cup bamboo shoots or baby corn (canned or fresh)
  - 1 cup snap peas or green beans (optional)
  - 1 cup sliced Thai eggplant or regular eggplant (optional)
- **For Serving:**
  - Cooked jasmine rice or steamed rice noodles
  - Lime wedges
  - Additional chopped basil or cilantro

Instructions:

1. Prepare the Curry Base:

1. **Heat Oil:**
   - In a large pot or Dutch oven, heat the vegetable oil over medium heat.
2. **Cook Curry Paste:**
   - Add the Thai green curry paste to the pot and sauté for 1-2 minutes, stirring constantly, until fragrant.

2. Cook Chicken:

1. **Add Chicken:**
   - Add the chicken pieces to the pot and cook, stirring occasionally, until they are no longer pink, about 4-5 minutes.
2. **Add Liquids:**
   - Pour in the coconut milk and chicken broth. Stir to combine and bring to a simmer.
3. **Season:**
   - Stir in the fish sauce, brown sugar, and bird chilies (if using). Add the kaffir lime leaves if you have them. Simmer for 10-15 minutes, or until the chicken is cooked through and tender.

3. Add Vegetables:

1. **Add Vegetables:**

- Add the sliced bell peppers, carrots, bamboo shoots, and any additional vegetables you are using. Simmer for another 5-7 minutes, or until the vegetables are tender but still crisp.
    2. **Finish with Herbs:**
        - Stir in the chopped fresh basil or cilantro.

4. Serve:

1. **Serve Over Rice:**
    - Serve the Thai green curry over jasmine rice or alongside steamed rice noodles.
2. **Garnish:**
    - Garnish with additional chopped basil or cilantro and lime wedges.

Tips:

- **Adjust Spice Level:** If you prefer a milder curry, start with 2 tablespoons of green curry paste and taste as you go. You can always add more if you like it spicier.
- **Vegetable Variations:** Feel free to customize the vegetables based on what you have available or your personal preferences.
- **Substitute Ingredients:** If you can't find Thai green curry paste, you can use red curry paste as an alternative, though it will change the flavor profile.

Enjoy your Thai Green Curry with Chicken! It's a fragrant, satisfying dish that's sure to bring a taste of Thailand to your table.

Spaghetti Carbonara

Ingredients:

- **For the Pasta:**
    - 12 ounces (340g) spaghetti
    - Salt (for the pasta water)
- **For the Sauce:**

- 4 ounces (115g) pancetta or thick-cut bacon, diced
- 2 large eggs
- 1 cup (100g) grated Pecorino Romano or Parmesan cheese (or a mix of both)
- 2 cloves garlic, minced (optional)
- Freshly ground black pepper, to taste
- 1 tablespoon olive oil (optional, for cooking pancetta or bacon)

Instructions:

1. Cook the Pasta:

1. **Boil Water:**
   - Bring a large pot of salted water to a boil.
2. **Cook Spaghetti:**
   - Add the spaghetti to the boiling water and cook according to the package instructions until al dente. Reserve 1 cup of pasta cooking water before draining.
3. **Drain Pasta:**
   - Drain the spaghetti and set aside.

2. Prepare the Sauce:

1. **Cook Pancetta/Bacon:**
   - In a large skillet over medium heat, cook the diced pancetta or bacon until crispy. If using, add the minced garlic in the last minute of cooking for additional flavor.
   - Remove the pancetta/bacon with a slotted spoon and set aside. Leave the rendered fat in the skillet.
2. **Prepare Egg Mixture:**
   - In a bowl, whisk together the eggs and grated cheese until well combined. Season with freshly ground black pepper.

3. Combine Ingredients:

1. **Mix Pasta and Pancetta/Bacon:**
   - Add the drained spaghetti to the skillet with the pancetta/bacon fat. Toss to coat the pasta in the fat and heat through.
2. **Add Egg Mixture:**
   - Remove the skillet from the heat. Quickly pour the egg and cheese mixture over the pasta, tossing vigorously to coat the spaghetti. The residual heat from the pasta and skillet will cook the eggs, creating a creamy sauce. If the sauce is too thick, add a little of the reserved pasta water, a tablespoon at a time, until you reach your desired consistency.
3. **Adjust Seasoning:**
   - Stir in the crispy pancetta/bacon and adjust seasoning with more black pepper if needed.

4. Serve:

1. **Plate the Pasta:**
   - Serve the Spaghetti Carbonara immediately, garnished with additional grated cheese and freshly ground black pepper if desired.

Tips:

- **Timing:** It's important to combine the egg mixture with the pasta off the heat to avoid scrambling the eggs. The heat from the pasta will cook the eggs gently and create a creamy sauce.
- **Cheese Choice:** Pecorino Romano gives a sharper, saltier flavor compared to Parmesan. You can use either or a blend of both based on your preference.
- **Pasta Water:** The starchy pasta water helps to achieve the right consistency for the sauce, so be sure to reserve some before draining.

Enjoy your Spaghetti Carbonara! It's a delicious and comforting dish that's perfect for a quick weeknight dinner or a special occasion.

Pumpkin Sage Risotto

Ingredients:

- **For the Risotto:**
    - 1 small pumpkin or 1 can (15 oz) pumpkin puree (not pumpkin pie filling)
    - 4 cups chicken or vegetable broth
    - 2 tablespoons olive oil or unsalted butter
    - 1 small onion, finely chopped

- 2 cloves garlic, minced
- 1 1/2 cups Arborio rice
- 1/2 cup dry white wine (optional, you can use extra broth if preferred)
- 1/2 cup grated Parmesan cheese
- 1/4 cup heavy cream (optional, for extra creaminess)
- Salt and black pepper, to taste
- **For the Sage:**
    - 2 tablespoons fresh sage leaves, finely chopped (or 1 teaspoon dried sage)
    - 2 tablespoons unsalted butter (for sage butter)
    - Extra sage leaves for garnish (optional)

Instructions:

1. Prepare the Pumpkin:

1. **Roast Pumpkin (if using fresh):**
   - Preheat the oven to 400°F (200°C).
   - Cut the pumpkin in half, remove seeds, and place cut-side down on a baking sheet.
   - Roast for 40-50 minutes, or until tender. Scoop out the flesh and mash or puree it. You should have about 1 cup of pumpkin puree.
   - If using canned pumpkin puree, just measure out 1 cup.

2. Prepare the Broth:

1. **Heat Broth:**
   - In a separate saucepan, keep the chicken or vegetable broth warm over low heat.

3. Make the Risotto:

1. **Sauté Aromatics:**
   - In a large skillet or pot, heat the olive oil or butter over medium heat.
   - Add the chopped onion and cook until translucent, about 5 minutes.
   - Stir in the minced garlic and cook for another 1 minute until fragrant.
2. **Cook Rice:**
   - Add the Arborio rice to the skillet, stirring to coat the rice with the oil and onions. Cook for 1-2 minutes until the edges of the rice become translucent.
3. **Deglaze:**
   - Pour in the white wine (if using) and cook, stirring constantly, until the wine is mostly absorbed by the rice.
4. **Add Broth:**
   - Begin adding the warm broth, 1/2 cup at a time, stirring constantly. Allow the liquid to be absorbed before adding more broth. This process takes about 18-20 minutes, and the rice should be creamy and al dente.

5. **Add Pumpkin and Sage:**
    - Stir in the pumpkin puree and chopped sage. Cook for an additional 2-3 minutes, allowing the flavors to meld.
6. **Finish Risotto:**
    - Stir in the Parmesan cheese and heavy cream (if using) for extra creaminess. Season with salt and black pepper to taste.

4. Prepare the Sage Butter:

1. **Make Sage Butter:**
    - In a small skillet, melt the butter over medium heat. Add the finely chopped sage and cook for 1-2 minutes until the sage becomes crispy and fragrant.

5. Serve:

1. **Plate the Risotto:**
    - Spoon the risotto onto plates or into bowls.
2. **Garnish:**
    - Drizzle with the sage butter and garnish with additional fresh sage leaves if desired.

Tips:

- **Consistency:** The risotto should be creamy but not too soupy. Adjust the amount of broth to achieve the desired consistency.
- **Stirring:** Constant stirring helps release the starches from the rice, creating a creamy texture.
- **Pumpkin Flavor:** If you want a more pronounced pumpkin flavor, you can add a bit of pumpkin spice or a pinch of nutmeg.

Enjoy your Pumpkin Sage Risotto! It's a rich, comforting dish that perfectly captures the flavors of the season.

Baked Chicken Parmesan

Ingredients:

- **For the Chicken:**
    - 4 boneless, skinless chicken breasts (pounded to an even thickness)
    - 1 cup all-purpose flour
    - 2 large eggs
    - 1 cup breadcrumbs (preferably panko for extra crunch)
    - 1/2 cup grated Parmesan cheese

- 1 teaspoon dried Italian seasoning or oregano
- 1/2 teaspoon garlic powder
- 1/2 teaspoon onion powder
- Salt and black pepper, to taste
- 2 tablespoons olive oil (for brushing)
- **For Topping:**
  - 1 1/2 cups marinara sauce
  - 1 cup shredded mozzarella cheese
  - 1/4 cup grated Parmesan cheese
  - Fresh basil or parsley, chopped (for garnish, optional)

Instructions:

1. Prepare the Chicken:

1. **Preheat Oven:**
   - Preheat your oven to 400°F (200°C). Line a baking sheet with parchment paper or lightly grease it.
2. **Prepare Breading Station:**
   - Set up a breading station with three shallow dishes:
     - **Flour:** Seasoned with salt and pepper.
     - **Eggs:** Lightly beaten.
     - **Breadcrumbs:** Mixed with 1/2 cup grated Parmesan cheese, Italian seasoning, garlic powder, onion powder, salt, and pepper.
3. **Bread Chicken:**
   - Dredge each chicken breast in the flour, shaking off excess.
   - Dip into the beaten eggs.
   - Coat with the breadcrumb mixture, pressing down gently to adhere.
4. **Arrange on Baking Sheet:**
   - Place the breaded chicken breasts on the prepared baking sheet. Brush the tops lightly with olive oil to help them crisp up during baking.

2. Bake the Chicken:

1. **Bake:**
   - Bake in the preheated oven for 20-25 minutes, or until the chicken is cooked through and the coating is golden and crispy. The internal temperature of the chicken should reach 165°F (74°C).

3. Add Toppings:

1. **Add Sauce and Cheese:**
   - Remove the chicken from the oven. Spoon about 3 tablespoons of marinara sauce over each piece of chicken.
   - Sprinkle shredded mozzarella cheese evenly over the sauce.

- Sprinkle with additional grated Parmesan cheese if desired.
  2. **Broil:**
     - Return the chicken to the oven and switch to the broiler setting. Broil for 2-3 minutes, or until the cheese is melted and bubbly. Watch closely to prevent burning.

4. Serve:

1. **Garnish:**
   - Garnish with chopped fresh basil or parsley if desired.
2. **Serve:**
   - Serve the Baked Chicken Parmesan over spaghetti or with a side of garlic bread and a simple green salad.

Tips:

- **Even Thickness:** Pounding the chicken breasts to an even thickness ensures that they cook evenly.
- **Crunchy Coating:** Panko breadcrumbs give a crispier texture, but regular breadcrumbs work well too.
- **Marinara Sauce:** Use a high-quality marinara sauce or homemade sauce for the best flavor.

Enjoy your Baked Chicken Parmesan! It's a comforting, classic dish that's easy to make and always a hit at the dinner table.

Roasted Garlic Mashed Potatoes

Ingredients:

- **For the Roasted Garlic:**
  - 1 whole head of garlic
  - 1 tablespoon olive oil
  - Salt and pepper, to taste
- **For the Mashed Potatoes:**
  - 2 pounds (900g) russet or Yukon Gold potatoes, peeled and cut into chunks

- 1/2 cup (120ml) milk or heavy cream
- 1/4 cup (60g) unsalted butter
- Salt and black pepper, to taste
- Fresh chives or parsley, chopped (for garnish, optional)

Instructions:

1. Roast the Garlic:

1. **Preheat Oven:**
   - Preheat your oven to 400°F (200°C).
2. **Prepare Garlic:**
   - Slice the top off the head of garlic to expose the cloves. Place the garlic on a piece of aluminum foil.
3. **Season and Roast:**
   - Drizzle olive oil over the exposed cloves and season with a pinch of salt and pepper.
   - Wrap the garlic in the foil and roast in the preheated oven for 35-40 minutes, or until the cloves are soft and caramelized.
4. **Cool and Squeeze:**
   - Let the garlic cool slightly. Squeeze the roasted cloves out of their skins and set aside.

2. Prepare the Potatoes:

1. **Boil Potatoes:**
   - Place the peeled and chopped potatoes in a large pot. Cover with cold water and add a pinch of salt.
   - Bring to a boil over medium-high heat and cook until the potatoes are tender, about 15-20 minutes.
2. **Drain Potatoes:**
   - Drain the potatoes well and return them to the pot. Let them sit for a minute or two to allow excess moisture to evaporate.

3. Mash the Potatoes:

1. **Heat Dairy:**
   - In a small saucepan, heat the milk or cream and butter over low heat until the butter is melted and the mixture is warm.
2. **Mash Potatoes:**
   - Mash the potatoes with a potato masher or use a potato ricer for a smoother texture.
3. **Incorporate Garlic:**
   - Add the roasted garlic cloves to the mashed potatoes. Mash or stir to combine.
4. **Add Dairy Mixture:**

- Gradually add the warm milk and butter mixture to the potatoes, stirring until the desired consistency is reached. You may not need all of the milk, so add it gradually.
5. **Season:**
   - Season the mashed potatoes with salt and black pepper to taste.

4. Serve:

1. **Garnish:**
   - Transfer the mashed potatoes to a serving dish and garnish with chopped fresh chives or parsley if desired.
2. **Serve Warm:**
   - Serve the Roasted Garlic Mashed Potatoes warm as a side dish with your favorite main course.

Tips:

- **Creamy Texture:** For extra creamy mashed potatoes, use a combination of milk and cream and make sure the dairy is warm when added.
- **Roasting Garlic:** You can roast garlic ahead of time and store it in the refrigerator for up to a week.
- **Avoid Over-Mashing:** Over-mashing potatoes can make them gluey. For the best texture, mash until smooth but not overworked.

Enjoy your Roasted Garlic Mashed Potatoes! They're a perfect, flavorful side dish that pairs well with a variety of main courses.

www.ingramcontent.com/pod-product-compliance
Lightning Source LLC
LaVergne TN
LVHW061943070526
838199LV00060B/3949